ROUGH MAGIC THEATRE COMPANY

MIDDEN

BY MORNA REGAN

MIDDEN

BY MORNA REGAN

CAST (in order of speaking)

DOPHIE	**BARBARA ADAIR**
RUTH	**KATHY DOWNES**
MA	**RUTH HEGARTY**
AILEEN	**PAULINE HUTTON**
MAB	**MAGGIE HAYES**

DIRECTOR	**LYNNE PARKER**
SET DESIGNER	**BLÁITHÍN SHEERIN**
COSTUME DESIGNER	**SINÉAD CUTHBERT**
LIGHTING DESIGNER	**TINA MacHUGH**
SOUND	**ALEXIS NEALON**
PRODUCTION MANAGER	**ANDY KEOGH**
STAGE DIRECTOR	**LYCETTE YUILL**
STAGE MANAGER	**PAMELA McQUEEN**
PRODUCTION ELECTRICIANS	**BARRY CONWAY, PAUL SPENCER**
COSTUME MAKER	**MARTIN ROBERTS**
HAIR & WIG STYLIST	**VAL SHERLOCK**
SET CONSTRUCTION	**THEATRE PRODUCTION SERVICES**
SCENE PAINTERS	**ORLA BASS, JENNIFER MOONAN**
GRAPHIC DESIGN	**ALPHABET SOUP**
PHOTOGRAPHY	**PAT REDMOND**
EDINBURGH PRESS REP.	**SALLY LYCETT**
ADMINISTRATIVE ASSISTANT	**ANNE-MARIE EVISTON**
PRODUCER	**DEBORAH AYDON**

MIDDEN was first performed at the Traverse Theatre, Edinburgh on 14th August 2001

The performance runs for approximately two hours and fifteen minutes, including one interval.

Please note that the text of the play which appears in this volume may be changed during the rehearsal process and appear in a slightly altered form in performance.

MIDDEN GLOSSARY

Midden –
- Short for kitchen midden (Middle English, of Scandinavian origin) – domestic refuse heap. In archaeology, this is the part of a dig which provides detailed insight into domestic life in the past
- Mess (in Derry vernacular, particularly in a domestic and sometimes emotional context)

The Angelus – Roman Catholic bells rung at noon and six pm

Bate – Derry prononciation of 'beat'

Beak – [pron. 'bake'] mouth or face

Boggin' – filthy, revolting

Feis – [pron. 'fesh'] competion of music, poetry, drama and Irish dancing

Grianán of Aileach – 5,000-year-old ringed fort on the Donegal/Derry border with wild and beautiful views

Gransha – local mental hospital in Derry

Heads and thraws – crammed in top-to-tail, like sardines

Jouk – look, peep

Lured – chuffed, delighted

Oul houl' the diddies – gossipy woman, arms folded under bosom [houl' = hold, diddies = breasts], in the style immortalised by Les Dawson

Spág – big, clumsy foot

Thon – that (used with gestures, as in 'thon size')

Thran – willful, stubborn

Wean – [pron 'wane'] child, baby, 'wee one'

Wee buns – easy-peasy, a cinch

Wile – (wild) very

The author wishes to thank the following for their support in the writing of this play: the Tyrone Guthrie Centre, Temple Bar Properties, Aidan Kelly, Dearbhla Regan, Lara Campbell, Loughlin Deegan, Pauline Hutton, Andrea Irvine, Rosaleen Linehan, Eileen McClosky, Eleanor Methven, Carol Moore and Matt and Mary Regan.

Rough Magic would like to thank the following for their support with this production: Aer Lingus, the Arts Council of Ireland, Dublin Corporation, Department of Foreign Affairs, the Abbey Theatre, CoisCéim Dance Theatre, Paul Costelloe, Costume, Opera Ireland, Stena, Tesco, all staff at the Traverse Theatre, Everyman Palace, Town Hall Theatre, Dublin Fringe Festival and Draíocht and Art of Dressing, by Kilkenny (Nassau St, Leopardstown and Kilkenny) - promoting Irish design.

MORNA REGAN WRITER

Morna Regan is from Derry City, Northern Ireland. She studied in London, and won a Fulbright Scholarship to the USA where she took a Masters in theatre at the University of Southern California. As an actor, she has worked at major theatres in Ireland, England and America. As a writer, her short film, **The Case of Majella McGinty**, won awards at film festivals in Cork, Derry, San Francisco, Cologne and Houston. **Midden** is her first play for the stage.

LYNNE PARKER DIRECTOR

Lynne is co-founder and Artistic Director of Rough Magic Theatre Company and an Associate Director of the Abbey Theatre.

Productions for Rough Magic include **Top Girls, Decadence, The Country Wife, Nightshade, Serious Money, Aunt Dan and Lemon, The Tempest, Lady Windermere's Fan, Digging For Fire, Love And A Bottle, I Can't Get Started, New Morning, Danti-Dan, Down Onto Blue, The Dogs, Hidden Charges, Halloween Night, The Way Of The World, Pentecost, Northern Star, The School for Scandal, The Whisperers, Boomtown, Three Days of Rain** and **Dead Funny.**

Work outside the company includes **The Trojan Women** (Peacock); **The Clearing** (Bush Theatre); **The Doctor's Dilemma** and **Tartuffe** (both Abbey Theatre); **The Playboy of the Western World, The Silver Tassie** and **Our Father** (Almeida Theatre); **Brothers of the Brush** (Arts Theatre); **The Shadow of a Gunman** (Gate); **Playhouse Creatures** (The Peter Hall Company at the Old Vic); **The Importance of Being Earnest** (West Yorkshire Playhouse); **Love Me?!** (Corn Exchange's Car Show) and **The Comedy of Errors** (Royal Shakespeare Company). She has also worked with a number of companies including Druid, Tinderbox, Opera Theatre Company and 7:84 Scotland and was an associate artist of Charabanc for whom she adapted and directed **The House of Bernarda Alba.** Future projects include Tom Murphy's **The Sanctuary Lamp** (Peacock Theatre) and Laura Ruohonen's **Olga**, translated by Linda McLean (Traverse Theatre, Edinburgh).

BARBARA ADAIR DOPHIE

Barbara created the part of Lily in Stewart Parker's **Pentecost** for Field Day and in the television adaptation. Her recent theatre credits include **The Old Lady's Guide to Survival** (Red Kettle) and many productions at the Lyric, Belfast, among them **Pygmalion, The Crucible, A Life** and **Juno and the Paycock.** Recent television includes **Beyond the Pale** and **Amongst Women**, and film includes **Eat the Peach** and **Divorcing Jack.**

KATHY DOWNES RUTH

Kathy's previous Rough Magic productions include **Northern Star** and **Boomtown.** Other theatre includes **The Tender Trap, Howling Moons Silent Sons, The Ash Fire, Jack Ketch's Gallows Jig** and **Red Roses and Petrol** (all Pigsback); **The Cavalcaders** (Theatr Clwyd); **Massive Damages** (Passion Machine); **Car Show** (Corn Exchange); **Judith** (Project); **Kissaway** (Semper Fi) and **Excitement** (Bewleys Café Theatre). TV includes **Growing Pains** (Littlebird); **Black Day At Blackrock** (Venus Films) and **Paths To Freedom** (Grand Pictures). Film includes **About Adam** (Venus) and **Bye Bye Inkhead** (Enzo Films).

MAGGIE HAYES MAB

Theatre includes **Troilus & Cressida** (Oxford Stage Company); **Northern Star** (Field Day); **All My Sons** (Arts Theatre); **The Merchant Of Venice** (Lyric Theatre); **The Evangelist** (Arts Theatre); **The Plough and The Stars** (American/Irish Tour); **The Poet And His Double** (Arts Theatre); **The Conduct of Life** (Regents Park); **Le Misanthrope** (Conservatoire de Rennes); **Les Mariés de la Tour Eiffel** (European Tour); **Exercises de Style** (CDR de Bretagne); **Paroles de Prévert** (Theatre des 3 Quartiers, Poitiers) and **Les Ruines de l'Empire** (Amphitheatre of Epidaurus). TV includes **Give My Head Peace, Citizenship** (both BBC) and **Trouble and Stryfe** (UTV). Film includes **The Most Fertile Man In Ireland** (Samson Films) and radio includes **Half Sketch, Half Biscuit** (BBC Radio 2).

RUTH HEGARTY MA

Ruth was born in Dublin and began her career at the Abbey Theatre. She has since worked in all the major theatres in Ireland, touring with the Irish Theatre Company in such shows as **Heartbreak House**. Ruth created the part of Daisy Bell in Stewart Parker's **Spokesong** and other theatre credits include **Educating Rita** (Gate); **Play It Again Sam** (Eblana Theatre); **Tarry Flynn** (Abbey); **The Communication Cord** (Field Day); **Brighton Beach Memoirs** (Andrews Lane/Red Kettle); **The Plough And The Stars** and **The Mayor Of Casterbridge** (both Second Age); **The Cavalcaders** (Theatr Clwyd); **Mackerel Sky** (Bush Theatre); **Juno And The Paycock** and **Mother Courage** (both Lyceum Theatre, Edinburgh); **Mackerel Sky** (Red Kettle), and the female version of **The Odd Couple** at Andrews Lane. Most recently Ruth played the part of Vera in Marie Jones's **Women On The Verge – Get A Life** at the Gaiety and on tour in the UK. Film and television work includes **The Life of JM Synge, Caught In A Free State, Strumpet City, The Ante Room, Eagles And Trumpets, Da, War Of The Buttons** and Glenroe.

PAULINE HUTTON AILEEN

Pauline is from Derry and trained at the Samuel Beckett Centre, Trinity College Dublin. Theatre work includes **Translations, Give Me Your Answer, Do!, Melonfarmer, The Chirpaun** and Katie Mitchell's production of **Iphigenia at Aulis** (Abbey & Peacock Theatres); **The Revengers Tragedy** (Loose Canon); **Romeo and Juliet** (Second Age); **The Lonesome West** (Druid); **Translations** (An Grianán Theatre); **The Whisperers** (Rough Magic); **Zoe's Play** (The Ark and Kennedy Center, Washington DC), and **Tea Set**, a one-woman show written by Gina Moxley and directed by Noeleen Kavanagh. Television and film work includes **Paths to Freedom, Glenroe, This is My Father, Double Carpet, Mad About Mambo, The Closer You Get, Postcards from the Hedge** and a short film entitled **Day One.**

DEBORAH AYDON PRODUCER

As Executive Producer of Rough Magic, Deborah has produced **The Whisperers, Boomtown, Three Days of Rain, Dead Funny,** two series of play readings under the banner of **Plays4**, and project managed the design and construction of the company's site-specific venue for the 1999 Dublin Theatre Festival. Deborah was General Manager of the Bush Theatre from 1991 to 1999, during which time the Bush developed and produced a prodigious range of new theatre writing. Highlights of this period include Billy Roche's **Wexford Trilogy;** Jonathan Harvey's **Beautiful Thing** (also national tour, Donmar and Duke of Yorks); Tracy Letts's **Killer Joe** (also West End); Joe Penhall's **Love and Understanding** (also Long Wharf Theater, New Haven, Ct); Conor McPherson's **This Lime Tree Bower** and **St Nicholas** (also New York), and Mark O'Rowe's **Howie the Rookie.**

SINÉAD CUTHBERT COSTUME DESIGNER

Sinéad is a costume designer and constructor. In the last eighteen months she has designed **How They Lied to Her Husband, Fishpond on Fire, Then They Were Married** and **Excitement** (all Bewley's Café Theatre); **L'Altro Mondo** (Opera Ireland); **Burn This** (Gúna Núa); **Blush** and **Over the Rainbow** (both Rex Levitates), and **Mutability** and **Richard III** (both Theatreworks). She is also Costume Supervisor for the Gate Theatre and Opera Ireland and works extensively for Dice Man street performance company. Sinéad won the Irish Times Best Costume Design Award 2000 for Mutability.

ANDY KEOGH PRODUCTION MANAGER

Previous productions include **Die Fledermaus** and **Madama Butterfly** (both Co-Opera); Ballet Ireland season 1999; Opera Ireland seasons 1999 - 2001, and Wexford Festival Opera 2000. Credits as production electrician include **Dancing At Lughnasa, The Secret Fall Of Constance Wilde** (Abbey); **Death And The Ploughman** (Project), and the **Pan Pan Theatre Symposium** (Samuel Beckett). Set construction credits include **Big Maggie** (Abbey); **An Ideal Husband** (Gate); **Beauty Queen of Leenane** (Gaiety); **Hot Press Music Awards** (BBC Northern Ireland); **Boomtown** (Rough Magic) and **A Month In The Country** (RSC).

TINA MacHUGH LIGHTING DESIGNER

Tina previously worked with Rough Magic on **The Whisperers** (Irish tour and Traverse), and her other extensive theatre credits include **The Wexford Trilogy** (Bush Theatre, Wexford and Peacock); **Hedda Gabler, Playboy of the Western World** and **The Hostage** (Abbey Theatre); **A Doll's House, Mother Courage** and **The House of Bernarda Alba** (Shared Experience); **Yard Gal** (Royal Court); **Love in a Wood, The Comedy of Errors, Ghosts, Henry VI, The Phoenician Women** and **Shadows** (RSC); **Rutherford and Son, The Machine Wreckers** and **Guiding Star** (Royal National Theatre); **Our Father** (Almeida); and **Spoonface Steinberg** (Sheffield Crucible/New Ambassadors). She was nominated for a Laurence Olivier Award for her work on Ghosts and Rutherford and Son. Tina also works regularly in opera and dance throughout Europe. Productions this year include **The Hunt For Red Willie** (Peacock), **Fragile** (Fabulous Beast Dance Theatre, Dublin) and **Nixon's Nixon** (Comedy).

PAMELA McQUEEN STAGE MANAGER

Pamela was Production Manager for **Rum & Vodka, The Good Thief, Much Ado About Nothing, Describe Joe** and **Why I Hate The Circus** for Greenlight Productions, of which she is a founder-member. Other production management includes the Dublin Fringe Festivals in 1999 and 2000, and stage management includes **When I Was God** (Everyman Palace); **Down The Line** (Peacock) and **Dead Funny** (Rough Magic). Pamela recently acted as Producer for the Greenlight/Project Summer School of Theatre Design.

BLÁITHÍN SHEERIN SET DESIGNER

Bláithín trained in sculpture and performance art at NCAD and in theatre design at Motley at Riverside Studios, London. Her designs for Rough Magic include **The Whisperers, The School for Scandal, Northern Star, Pentecost, The Way of the World, The Dogs, Digging for Fire** and **Love and a Bottle**. Other design credits include **Eden, As the Beast Sleeps, You Can't Take it with You** and **Made in China** (Abbey and Peacock); **The Comedy of Errors** (RSC); **Our Father** (Almeida Theatre); **The Importance of Being Earnest** (West Yorkshire Playhouse); **Juno and the Paycock** (Lyric Theatre); composite set design for **The Beckett Festival** (Gate Theatre and John Jay Theatre, New York), and **The Fourth Wise Man** (Ark). She has also designed for Druid, Groundwork, Charabanc, Red Kettle, TEAM, Second Age, Fishamble, Galloglass and Prime Cut theatre companies and was Design Consultant on **Alice's Adventures in Wonderland/Alice Through the Looking Glass** (Blue Raincoat/Peacock Partners).

LYCETTE YUILL STAGE DIRECTOR

Lycette trained at UUC and spent 3 years with Sculpture Theatre Company, Birmingham. Previous Rough Magic productions include **Three Days of Rain** and **Dead Funny**. Other theatre credits include **Philadelphia Here I Come!** and **The Lonesome West** (both Druid); **Diamonds In The Soil** and **The Lost Days Of Ollie Deasey** (both Macnas); **The Dead School** (Macnas/Galway Arts Festival); **The Odyssey** (Macnas/Els Comedients); **Moll** (Edward Farrell Productions); **SITE** (Fir Clis & Galway Arts Festival); **Translations** (An Grianán) and **Dealer's Choice** (Prime Cut).

MIDDEN on tour 2001

14th - 25th August	Traverse Theatre, Edinburgh (Edinburgh Festival Fringe)
29th August - 1st September	Playhouse Theatre, Derry
4th - 8th September	Everyman Palace, Cork
11th - 15th September	Town Hall Theatre, Galway
8th - 13th October	Draíocht Centre for the Arts Blanchardstown, Dublin 15 (Dublin Fringe Festival)

FOR ROUGH MAGIC

ARTISTIC DIRECTOR LYNNE PARKER
EXECUTIVE PRODUCER DEBORAH AYDON
LITERARY MANAGER LOUGHLIN DEEGAN
ADMINISTRATOR CIARA Mc GLYNN

BOARD OF DIRECTORS

MARK MORTELL (CHAIR)
PAUL BRADY
MARIE BREEN
CATHERINE DONNELLY
DARRAGH KELLY
JOHN McGOLDRICK
PAULINE McLYNN
JOHN O'DONNELL

ADVISORY COUNCIL

SIOBHÁN BOURKE
ANNE BYRNE
DECLAN HUGHES
DARRAGH KELLY
PAULINE McLYNN
HÉLÈNE MONTAGUE
MARTIN MURPHY
ARTHUR RIORDAN
STANLEY TOWNSEND

ROUGH MAGIC THEATRE COMPANY
5/6 South Great Georges Street
Dublin 2 • Ireland
Tel: + 353 1 6719278
Fax: + 353 1 6719301
Email: roughmag@iol.ie

Reg No: 122753

Rough Magic gratefully acknowledges the support of the Arts Council of Ireland,
Dublin Corporation, the Department of Foreign Affairs and our Patrons.

ROUGH MAGIC THEATRE COMPANY

Rough Magic is one of Ireland's leading new writing companies. Since its formation in 1984, the company has combined world premières of new Irish plays with Irish premières of work from the contemporary international scene. This international perspective is a guiding principle of the company's approach to new work.

NEW WRITERS

This debut play by Morna Regan was commissioned by Rough Magic as part of our long-established work with new writers. Writers' debuts with Rough Magic have included Declan Hughes, Gina Moxley and Donal O'Kelly, and eight of these debut plays were recently published in a single volume (Rough Magic: First Plays, New Island, 1999). The company's commissioning programme has now been expanded through a new initiative in conjunction with the Dublin Fringe Festival - **SEEDS** - which aims to seek out, encourage, enable, develop and stage new Irish writing. A painstaking selection process whittled down over 100 submissions to arrive at six emerging writers who are now writing a new play to commission. These writers will be provided with resources for workshops, travel and research, and will be mentored (by directors who are highly experienced in working with new plays), to help guide their progress at this early stage in their careers. These plays will be presented in a platform event in Dublin in the spring of 2002.

INTERNATIONAL TOURING

MIDDEN had its world première at the Traverse Theatre, Edinburgh, as part of the Edinburgh Festival Fringe 2001. This production follows many Rough Magic productions which have toured to major new writing houses in the UK. The first of these was Declan Hughes's **DIGGING FOR FIRE** in 1992, which won great acclaim and a Time Out Award when presented at the Bush Theatre, London. This relationship continued with a co-production of Declan Hughes's next piece, **NEW MORNING,** in 1993. Rough Magic productions subsequently played at Hampstead Theatre, the Donmar Warehouse and the Tricycle Theatre, and several shows have visited the Edinburgh Festival, most recently **THE WHISPERERS** in 1999. Rough Magic productions have also played in Australia, New Zealand, and the USA: most recently the highly acclaimed American première of Stewart Parker's **PENTECOST** at the Island: Arts from Ireland Festival at the Kennedy Center, Washington DC in May 2000.

IMPORTS

In parallel to this export of Irish work, Rough Magic is committed to bringing work from the contemporary international scene to Ireland. In the last twelve months, this has included full productions of Richard Greenberg's **THREE DAYS OF RAIN** and Terry Johnson's **DEAD FUNNY,** and public readings of work by Joe Penhall, Shelagh Stephenson, Michel Tremblay, Helen Edmundson, Michael Wall and Michael Frayn.

THE FUTURE

Work in development and under commission includes the six new plays which form the **SEEDS** project, new pieces from Elizabeth Kuti **(THE WHISPERERS)** and Gina Moxley **(DANTI-DAN),** and a radical new piece of music theatre by Arthur Riordan and Bell Helicopter.

ROUGH MAGIC PRODUCTIONS

WP = World Première   IP = Irish Première

1984

TALBOT'S BOX
by Thomas Kilroy
FANSHEN
by David Hare – IP
THE BIG HOUSE
by Brendan Behan
THIRST
by Myles na gCopaleen

DECADENCE
by Steven Berkoff – IP
SEXUAL PERVERSITY IN CHICAGO
by David Mamet
TOP GIRLS
by Caryl Churchill – IP
AMERICAN BUFFALO
by David Mamet

1985

TOP GIRLS
by Caryl Churchill
SEXUAL PERVERSITY IN CHICAGO
by David Mamet
VICTORY
by Howard Barker – IP
NO END OF BLAME
by Howard Barker – IP

THE ONLY JEALOUSY OF EMER
by WB Yeats
MIDNITE AT THE STARLITE
by Michael Hastings – IP
CAUCASIAN CHALK CIRCLE
by Bertolt Brecht

1986

MIDNITE AT THE STARLITE
by Michael Hastings
CAUCASIAN CHALK CIRCLE
by Bertolt Brecht
BETRAYAL
by Harold Pinter – IP
**DOGG'S HAMLET, CAHOOT'S
MACBETH**
by Tom Stoppard
DECADENCE
by Steven Berkoff

AUNT DAN AND LEMON
by Wallace Shawn – IP
BLOODY POETRY
by Howard Brenton
THE COUNTRY WIFE
by William Wycherly
THE WOMAN IN WHITE
adapted from Wilkie Collins's
novel – IP

1987

NIGHTSHADE
by Stewart Parker
ROAD
by Jim Cartwright – IP
THE TEMPEST
by Shakespeare

THE SILVER TASSIE
by Sean O'Casey
A MUG'S GAME
adaptation of Le Bourgeois
Gentilhomme and Everyman – IP

1988

THE WHITE DEVIL
by John Webster – IP
TOM AND VIV
by Michael Hastings – IP
**TEA AND SEX AND
SHAKESPEARE**
a new version by Thomas Kilroy

BAT THE FATHER RABBIT THE SON
by Donal O'Kelly – WP
SERIOUS MONEY
by Caryl Churchill – IP

1989

BAT THE FATHER RABBIT THE SON
by Donal O'Kelly
A HANDFUL OF STARS
by Billy Roche – IP

SPOKESONG
by Stewart Parker
OUR COUNTRY'S GOOD
by Timberlake Wertenbarker – IP

1990

LADY WINDERMERE'S FAN
by Oscar Wilde
I CAN'T GET STARTED
by Declan Hughes – WP

BAT THE FATHER RABBIT THE SON
by Donal O'Kelly

1991

LOVE AND A BOTTLE
by George Farquhar, adapted by
Declan Hughes - WP
LADY WINDERMERE'S FAN
by Oscar Wilde

I CAN'T GET STARTED
by Declan Hughes
DIGGING FOR FIRE
by Declan Hughes - WP

1992

DIGGING FOR FIRE
by Declan Hughes
BAT THE FATHER RABBIT THE SON
by Donal O'Kelly
LOVE AND A BOTTLE
by George Farquhar, adapted by
Declan Hughes

THE DOGS
by Donal O'Kelly - WP
THE EMERGENCY SESSION
by Arthur Riordan - WP

1993

NEW MORNING
by Declan Hughes - WP

THE WAY OF THE WORLD
by William Congreve

1994

LADY WINDERMERE'S FAN
by Oscar Wilde
DOWN ONTO BLUE
by Pom Boyd - WP

HIDDEN CHARGES
by Arthur Riordan - WP

1995

DANTI-DAN
by Gina Moxley - WP

PENTECOST
by Stewart Parker

1996

PENTECOST
by Stewart Parker

NORTHERN STAR
by Stewart Parker

1997

HALLOWEEN NIGHT
by Declan Hughes - WP

MRS. SWEENEY
by Paula Meehan - WP

1998

THE SCHOOL FOR SCANDAL
by Richard Brinsley Sheridan

1999

THE WHISPERERS
Frances Sheridan's *'A Trip To Bath'* as
completed by Elizabeth Kuti - WP

BOOMTOWN
by Pom Boyd, Declan Hughes and
Arthur Riordan - WP

2000

PENTECOST
by Stewart Parker

THREE DAYS OF RAIN
by Richard Greenberg - IP
PLAYS[4] - public play readings

2001

DEAD FUNNY
by Terry Johnson - IP
PLAYS[4] - public play readings

MIDDEN
by Morna Regan - WP

ROUGH MAGIC PATRONS

Rough Magic is approved for tax-deductible sponsorship under Section 32 of the Finance Act 1984. If you would like to become a Rough Magic Patron, please contact us on + 353 (0) 1 671 9278 or at roughmag@iol.ie.

MIDDEN

Morna Regan

For Rónán

grá

Characters

in order of appearance

DOPHIE, *early 70s*
RUTH, *early 30s*
MA, *early 50s*
AILEEN, *mid to late 20*s
MAB, *early 30s*

The play is set in the kitchen area of a modest semi-d, in Derry City, Northern Ireland. It takes place in the present day.

PART ONE

Scene One

It is the middle of the night. A pale light is switched on in the stairwell, spilling on to the set. Enter DOPHIE, *agitated. She goes to the sink and turns the taps on, losing herself for a moment in the sensation.*

DOPHIE (*like the sound of the sea in a shell*). Ssshhh . . .

Calmer now, she turns them off, sits down at the table and waits. Agitation builds again. Out a window in the fourth wall she traces the journey of a car along the street. She gets up and tries the back door but can't open it. She gives it a last useless thump.

(*A warning thrown up the stairs.*) I could huff and puff and *blow* this house down.

Pacing.

Where are you lamb? Hurry up. (*Pause.*) It's very late in the day for us now.

DOPHIE *is at the fourth wall window. Behind her, a head appears at the glass panel of the back door. And then at the back window.*

Very late.

The handle of the back door is rattled futilely and the door thumped again. DOPHIE *takes herself to the bottom of the stairs to watch as the kitchen window opens and a body squeezes itself in over the sink and into the room. Her heart lifts visibly as* RUTH *lands on her honkers.*

RUTH (*staying close to the floor*). Oh God I could kiss you! Except I won't. I peed there once. (*Laughing then slumping, she pulls her knees up.*) I wish I was four again.

DOPHIE. And still be peeing on the floor?

RUTH (*startled*). What?. . . Oh my God, Dophie!

DOPHIE. You can come home, but none of us can go back. (*Pause.*) Thank God.

RUTH. Right now I just want to crawl under a stone.

DOPHIE (*with open arms*). Here, get in under me oxter so.

RUTH *goes to her and they hug.*

RUTH. You smell exactly the same as you always did. Baby powder. Now I know I'm home. I could sleep standing here. Do you remember the time you sent me out for some and I came back with the bottle of Baby Powers?

Beat.

This is just where I wanted to be all along.

DOPHIE. I know. All I wanted too.

RUTH. And if I'd been let stay I wouldn't be in this bloody mess now, would I? (*Trying not to cry.*) Oh Dophie, I've made such an incredible mess –

DOPHIE. There shush pet –

RUTH. The Ma must think I'm *insane*. Everybody –

DOPHIE. Ssh. Don't you worry about her, I'll buffer you this time. This time I promise. This time lamb. Sshh. . .

RUTH (*breaking the embrace*). Well bloody pity about her. It's as much her fault as mine that she has this landing on her doorstep. Isn't it? So she can just deal with it! Sorry. I haven't slept for weeks. (*Pause.*) I better see about getting my bags in. You're up very late, how come?

DOPHIE. I was waiting for you.

RUTH (*surprised*). You were?

DOPHIE. I could feel you getting closer to me.

Beat.

RUTH (*laughing*). Like a bad rain coming.

She opens the door to get her bags.

RUTH. It's a lot easier getting out of this house than it is getting in.

She steps out.

DOPHIE. I don't know what I've been at all my life then.

RUTH *steps in again with two heavy bags, a matching vanity case, and a portfolio.* DOPHIE *takes the little vanity case off her.*

(*Whispering.*) Here, let me help you.

RUTH (*struggling with the rest of the bags to the bottom of the stairs*). Thanks. Why are we whispering?

DOPHIE. You don't want her down do you?

RUTH. No. I suppose I don't. Tomorrow's time enough for that. Time to get my guard back up.

DOPHIE *flicks the light off and follows her up the stairs.*

(*Off-stage.*) She used to leave the key over the door.

DOPHIE (*off-stage*). She used to do a lot of things. She's spent all that money.

RUTH (*off-stage*). She's what?

DOPHIE (*off-stage*). Well that's the only thing I can think of. Did you bring me bon-bons?

RUTH (*off-stage*). Bon-bons?

It peters out.

Scene Two

Lights up. It is the afternoon of the following day. MA *bustles in through the back door with four or five bags of shopping.*

MA. Aileen! Come down and give us a hand with these would you? Aileen!! (*She takes off a head scarf, and pushes up her hair.*) Aileen!!!

AILEEN *comes down the stairs.*

MA. AILEEN! (*Seeing her.*) Oh, sorry. I'm way behind myself pet. Did she ring? (AILEEN *shakes her head.*)Ah well. God knows what another phone-call would bring. That last one was just a gem. (*Filling a kettle.*)What time is it? I'd need to be getting the roast ready before we set sail and I have to –

AILEEN. You've bags of time. Calm yourself woman.

MA. I am calm.

AILEEN (*from one of the bags*). Champagne!? La-di-da!

MA (*taking it off her*). Don't be shaking that up for God's sake Aileen, have you no nous? That's good.

AILEEN *smirks. She knows her rot-gut.*

(*Putting it in the fridge.*) How was the Mammy for you?

AILEEN. She's out for the count. Did you get your hair done?

MA. Not really.

AILEEN. You either did or you didn't.

MA. I'm not surprised she's sleeping the day out. I heard the pair of youse up clattering about in the middle of the night. What was it this time?

AILEEN. Dunno. Wee-wees probably.

MA. The critter. She has herself wound up to high doh as well. Maybe I shouldn't have said anything.

AILEEN. My God, feel the weight of this. (*She lifts a hefty cut of meat out of one of the bags.*) Fatted calf for the prodigal daughter. She'll love that.

MA. Dress it and put it in the pan would you? Make yourself useful.

AILEEN *goes to.* MA *goes to the hot-cupboard and takes out a tablecloth wrapped in tissue-paper.*

I always love the smell of this. It smells gracious. Smells like Christmas or something.

AILEEN. The Christmas you sent our Ruth up to her room for spilling red wine all over it?

MA. I did no such thing.

AILEEN. Sorry. I forgot. Of course you didn't.

MA *starts setting the table.*

MA. Four place settings again. It's a long time since I've had all my people gathered around the one table. (*Pause.*) Well as many as is humanly possible to gather anyway. I just wish it could be under happier circumstances.

AILEEN. It is happy.

MA. Oh aye, ecstatic. No man could bear it.

AILEEN. Would you stop? It's what Ruth wants. She always said it's what she wants.

DOPHIE (*off-stage*). Miss?

MA. Yes? (*To* AILEEN.) What must they be thinking over there? It'll be all over the papers over there you know.

AILEEN. Maybe you should just be thinking about Ruth.

MA. Do you think I'm not? She has me up the walls.

MA *wets tea.*

Enter DOPHIE.

DOPHIE (*cranky*). Miss?

MA. Are you not dead yet?

AILEEN. Mammy.

MA (*to* DOPHIE). Yes?

DOPHIE. I'm very dry.

AILEEN. Nana, I put you over. Can you still not sleep?

DOPHIE (*to* MA, *seating herself*). Milk and one sugar, please.

MA (*giving it to her*). Sure I know how you take your tea.

DOPHIE. Thank you very much.

MA. You're very welcome.

　　DOPHIE *starts to stroke the table cloth.* MA *watches her.*

(*Gently.*) Do you recognise it Mammy?

　　DOPHIE *strokes it a moment longer, then stops.*

Do you Mammy? Look at it.

Beat.

Here. Take it in your hand. Please.

But the moment is gone. DOPHIE *is staring hard out the window.*

It's all right. Never mind. (*Smoothing* DOPHIE*'s hair.*)
I bought you a wee perm lotion up the town. Maybe I'll set
your hair for you later on? Eh?

MA *gives* DOPHIE *a kiss on the top of her head and leaves.*
DOPHIE *shirks off any vestige of the kiss.*

(*To* AILEEN.) I thought we had her there for a minute.

AILEEN (*putting away groceries*). Look at this. After Eights?
And a *Battenberg!* Jesus you'd think it was Royalty was
coming. What did you get me?

MA. Sure aren't you just the wee dog we always had.

　　AILEEN *laughs.* DOPHIE *is rubbing at the tablecloth,
agitated.* MA *is rummaging inside the hot-cupboard.*

Half past should leave us plenty of time to get to the airport,
shouldn't it? Are you getting dressed at all today Mammy?
Here put this on you.

*She hangs a blue dress on the door and goes back in for
tights, underwear etc.*

DOPHIE (*going for the sink*). There's no need.

MA. For going to the airport.

DOPHIE. There's no need.

MA. It's your favourite. Don't give me a handling.

DOPHIE (*turning on the taps*). Woman I'm telling you, there's no need.

AILEEN. Watch.

MA (*sharply*). Mammy! (*She gets absolutely drenched trying to turn the taps off.*) Jesus Christ, Mam-my!!

RUTH *appears in the stairwell, dressed in a casual chic trouser suit and carrying a bag. The air about her is more collected now, although the effort to keep it so is apparent. She stops when she sees what is going on and, unseen by the others, witnesses the following –*

MA *– a reflex action – slaps* DOPHIE *hard on the wrist.* RUTH *and* DOPHIE *recoil simultaneously.*

Ah now look what you made me do! What is it with those bloody taps? They are the bane of my life.

AILEEN. It's all right Dophie. Come here.

MA. You'll scald yourself one of these days. Or drown yourself. Do you hear me?

AILEEN. Mammy –

DOPHIE *is trying to get the hot-cupboard door open.*

MA. If I don't do it for you! Where are you going now?

DOPHIE. Up.

MA. That way. And you're coming to the airport.

DOPHIE *heads for the stairs.*

DOPHIE. We'll see about that.

MA. Ah go on, go. You have me demented.

AILEEN (*handing her her dress as she passes – gently*). Here take this with you Nana. I'll be up in a minute. Mammy, you need to calm yourself.

MA (*flaring at* DOPHIE *again*). This is all your doing, you know. It was *you* started all this. (DOPHIE *flinches in fear of another slap.*) Do you hear me?!

AILEEN. Mammy.

MA. Well it's coming back to visit you now, isn't it? About to walk off a plane to visit both of us. *Isn't* it?

Exit DOPHIE.

MA. No wonder the woman can't sleep.

RUTH *tries to intercept* DOPHIE *on the stairs but she just wants up.*

AILEEN. What have you got yourself so het up over Mammy?

MA. Allow me to be het up, Aileen. Honest to God, what does that wee girl think she's playing at anyway? One minute she can't even make the time to come home for the launch, and the next we know she's on her way back for good. And whatever about us, what sort of a position has she left Mab McGinty in, I would like to know?

AILEEN. I'm sure the two of them have something sorted out. Mabs McGinty is no fool when it comes to business and our Ruth is a –

MA. – genius. Sure our Ruth's a genius. She must be. Three days to 'sort out' a business that took them over ten years to build. Anyone with a head on them would have themselves settled by now. Instead of buckin' it all away in what looks to me for all intents and purposes like the middle of a nervous break-down. Or worse, a whim.

RUTH *turns and walks back up the stairs.*

Everything she has going for her. *He* didn't get much notice either, did he? What does she think she's coming back to anyway? (*Touching her hair.*) Museum pieces? Maybe he was taking a swipe? Or embezzling or something like that?

RUTH *stops.*

MA. Maybe she'd good reason to walk.

AILEEN. I'm sure she had. Just don't go lighting into her as soon as her plane hits the tarmac.

Beat.

MA. I'm surprised she hasn't been over to see us yet.

AILEEN. Who? Mab?

MA. She's back a fortnight.

AILEEN. Up to her teeth probably. Sure she's the launch practically on top of her.

MA. Aye. Landed *right* in it, wasn't she? (*Lifting up* DOPHIE*'s cup.*) Look. She didn't even touch the tea she came down for. Bring it up to her would you Aileen, and a bit of the Battenberg as well. Oh here, I'll bring it up myself. A peace offering. And get yourself dressed – we'll never be out the door.

AILEEN. Dressed?

> RUTH *decides to take the bull by the horns and sashays into the fray.*

RUTH. Not on my account I hope.

MA. Sweet Lamb of God!

AILEEN. *Ruth?!!*

RUTH. In the flesh.

MA. Jesus! What else has she in store for us? What are you doing here?

RUTH. Well I'm not selling coal, Mammy. Don't all rush at me at once!

MA. But we're on our way to the airport –

RUTH (*open arms for her Mother*). Well then I saved you a trip.

MA. You might have . . . How'd you –

RUTH. I got lucky with an earlier connection.

MA. You're one head-stagger after the other.

RUTH. My arms are getting sore.

> MA *still can't move.* AILEEN *nips in and embraces* RUTH.

AILEEN. Welcome home sister! God I can't believe it. What are you like, you mentalist?! Look at the swank of her.

RUTH (*laughing*). I suppose you'll be back to raiding my wardrobe.

AILEEN. In the door two minutes and she's still on about her yellow flares I burst when I was ten.

> RUTH *laughs. It dissolves into an awkwardness between her and* MA.

RUTH. The place seems tiny. I feel like Alice in Wonderland.

MA. Are you going somewhere?

RUTH (*confused*). Where would I be going?

AILEEN. You're wile dressed up.

MA. And the bag.

RUTH. Oh, that's presents.

AILEEN. Way-hey, loot!

RUTH. I'm not going anywhere Mammy. I just got home. Am I getting a hug or what?

MA. I'll soak your good suit.

RUTH. It'll survive.

MA. Welcome home, of course darling. You just caught me off guard. Here.

They hug.

(*Softly.*) What's happening with you Ruth?

RUTH. God Mammy, you've shrunk.

MA. Well daughter, that's what happens. And sure look at you – all grown up. We've nearly twice as much of you back as we sent away.

RUTH. I haven't put on any weight. I'm exactly the same weight for the past ten years.

MA. Well how's your Mammy supposed to know that?

RUTH. Well didn't my Mammy get plenty of invites to come out and see me? You could have come any time with Aileen –

MA. And leave your Nana? You could have been home more often.

RUTH. And leave the business?

MA. Mabs managed it.

RUTH. Mabs is different.

MA. How so? A couple of Christmases in nearly fifteen years Ruth. And now out of the blue you just –

AILEEN. Girls. Girls.

They back down.

RUTH. I told you why Mammy. I just thought that if I kept my nose to the grindstone, the quicker I'd be able to get back for *good.* You even said that yourself. I just didn't think it would take so bloody long. (*Pause.*) I hated it there.

MA. Hmmn. How'd you get here anyway?

RUTH. I took a taxi.

MA. From the airport? You took a taxi all the way from the airport? How much did that cost you?

RUTH. Sixty quid. Sixty something –

MA. Jesus Mary and Joseph, Ruth. That's obscene. And us sitting here ready to come and get you.

AILEEN. Girls –

RUTH *keeps her tongue bitten.*

MA. It's well seeing you're not scrubbing floors for it. (*Pause.*) Anyway you're home now.

AILEEN. Returned at last to the land of milk and honey.

MA. You never did have any respect for money.

RUTH (*sword drawn*). What is that supposed to mean?

AILEEN. Honest to God, I'm going to SuperBites for my tea if this keeps up.

They back off.

Beat.

RUTH. You put up new wall-paper.

MA. I had to do something. Those walls hadn't been touched in over twenty years.

AILEEN. Right enough, they were boggin'. They'd gone a lovely shade of 'nicotine and chip fat'.

RUTH. I liked it.

MA. You didn't have to look at it everyday.

RUTH. No. No, I didn't.

AILEEN. Well you can like the new stuff too. I nearly broke me back getting it done 'before our Ruthie gets back'.

MA. All the notice we got.

RUTH. You didn't have to redecorate for me. I stencilled the old border. Remember? That was a wee piece of me. Those sunflowers.

MA. Sure they'd long since faded into oblivion.

AILEEN. Mammy, it would help if we'd a few less of the barbs.

MA. It would help if I'd a few more of the blanks filled in. Ruth –

RUTH. Where's Dophie? Is she all right?

MA (*thrown*). Of course she's all right. Why wouldn't she be? Probably still sleeping.

RUTH. Probably.

AILEEN. Give us wur pressies then!

MA. Aileen Josephine Eva Sweeney!

RUTH. Outside zip. Hoke away.

> AILEEN *opens the bag, takes out a plastic bag and out of that starts lifting out three beautifully store-wrapped boxes and placing them on the table.*

MA. Ruth?

No reply.

> It's an awful lot to throw away on a split second decision Ruth.

RUTH. It wasn't split second.

MA. What then? You took him on a long slow meander up the garden path?

RUTH. Jesus Mammy, I'm not *made* of steel you know.

MA (*backing off*). Tell me then Ruth. I'm sorry.

RUTH. I don't think you'd understand.

MA. Really. You think my world is that minuscule?

RUTH. Well you were certainly never thrown out to the far end of it.

MA. And neither were you my dear.

RUTH. Oh was I not?

MA. Ruth for God's sake grow up. What happened to you?

RUTH. Easy. Mammy. Just sitting at an intersection the other day on my way to work and I came to my senses. I saw these two oul paddies, the big wide hairy faces on them and the suits, the flat caps, the works, blathering away for all the world as if they were still hanging over a fence in Donegal, instead of hanging over the giant pink claw of a dinosaur-shaped shopping mall. Eating *Tacobell*. I caught a line as I drove past. 'And what the fuck would Socrates know about electricity?' What the fuck would Socrates know about electricity, hey? Smart men. But so out of context. So maybe not that smart. And I looked at them and just thought 'Right that's it. I am outta here. I'm going home.' And drove off. Simple as that. It was the first time in a long time that anything I had decided to do actually made any sense to me. (*To* AILEEN.) Are you not going to open them?

AILEEN. I was waiting for an appropriate lull.

MA. It doesn't really answer my question.

RUTH. It does you know. Completely answers it.

MA. But what about the wedding Ruth?

AILEEN. I haven't seen a flat-capper in Donegal for years. They're all wearing base-ball caps.

RUTH. Really?

AILEEN. And we have tacos now too you know.

MA. I guess it's just as well then I hadn't forked out for the plane tickets yet.

RUTH *looks horrified.*

AILEEN (*reading the generic label on one of the boxes*). 'Mom'. Dear God. Do we have one of those?

RUTH (*embarrassed*). I know. They were wrapped in the factory store. Shop, I mean.

AILEEN. There you are Mommie dearest.

MA. Thank you Ruth. You shouldn't have.

AILEEN (*tearing into it*). Course she should.

MA. Don't be wasting the good paper, Aileen.

AILEEN (*unwrapping now with exaggerated meticulousness*). Sorry.

RUTH. Does my voice sound loud to you? In here?

AILEEN. Eh?

MA (*unwrapping a beautiful pink lace camisole and French knickers*). Oh Ruth, your sewing is beautiful. The detail. Look. These are *gorgeous*. They must have taken you hours.

RUTH (*embarrassed*). Well, actually I only designed them. They're part of our latest range. We've started doing lingerie to compliment the clothes. I finished the embroidery myself though. And look. Wait till you see this.

MA (*studying where RUTH has turned the hem over*). What? Oh no, look. What's that? Do you want me to get you a needle and thread?

RUTH. No of course not. That's on purpose. (*Laughing.*) That's Dophie's three slipped stitches.

MA. Dophie's what?

RUTH. Her three slipped stitches. You must remember that. She showed me when I was thon size at her knee. 'A planned mistake daughter so you don't challenge God's pride by creating perfection'. She was fierce about it too. 'The best finish you can put on anything.'

AILEEN. I certainly never heard that before.

MA. Sure what would she be telling you for? You couldn't be got to thread a needle even if the knickers were hanging off you. But I don't think I ever heard it before either Ruth. I would remember that.

RUTH. Dophie'll know what it is.

MA (*refolding her present carefully*). I'll have to put these away somewhere.

RUTH. Mammy I made them for you to wear. Not to be left lying in some drawer.

MA. I'd rather keep them. Sure where would I get to wear the likes of these at my age?

RUTH *looks ticked.*

AILEEN. Aye right enough. The wrapping paper'll probably come in handier. (*Unwrapping an exquisite boned basque.*) Now this'll *definitely* be put to good use. This is the business, Ruth. Very sexy – (*Vamping it up to Big Spender.*) De de de de de, de ne ne, dah da!

MA. Peel some spuds there Aileen. Might as well get the show on the road, seeing as you're here now.

RUTH. Can I give you a hand with anything? What's the smell?

AILEEN. Fatted calf.

MA (*putting it in the oven*). It is the very best of milk-finished Irish lamb.

RUTH (*to* AILEEN). Sure she knows I haven't eaten meat in nearly twenty years.

AILEEN. Well she thinks it's about time you outgrew that phrase. Just move it about your plate a bit and make all the right noises and you'll be grand. Pass us some napkins there.

RUTH. Napkins?

AILEEN. If the woman wants napkins, surely we can do the napkin thing?

RUTH (*getting them*). I feel like a visitor. (*Clearing the remnants of wrapping paper, bags, labels etc.*) Want anything here or will I put it all in the garbage?

MA. The *garbage!* Would you listen to her!

AILEEN (*American accent*). Sure thing sis, trash-can's right over there.

RUTH. I meant the bin. (*Defensive.*) You never wear anything I make you Mammy. Why wouldn't you let me design you something to wear to the launch?

MA. I thought you'd enough on your plate making us all stuff for the wedding. (*Beat.*)

RUTH. Oh.

AILEEN is ready to referee again. Enter DOPHIE. She has put on the blue dress. The lining is hanging down and her hair is a mess. RUTH has to hide how disconcerted she is at the sight of her.

Dophie! Reinforcements at last.

DOPHIE *stares at her blankly.*

Nana, it's me.

MA *tries to smooth down her dress and tuck her in.*

MA. Are you all right Mammy?

It is an apology of sorts. DOPHIE ignores her and continues staring blankly at RUTH.

RUTH. Dophie?

Beat.

Suddenly, as if a light has just come on, DOPHIE makes straight for her with open arms.

DOPHIE. Oh lamb. It *is* you! I knew it was you. I *knew* you were coming.

MA. My god, there's salt in the old dog yet.

DOPHIE. I could *feel* it.

MA. Sure we've been telling you all week Mammy.

DOPHIE (*hand on her chest*). Right through here. Come here to me.

DOPHIE *embraces* RUTH *and they shuffle round.*

You've come back. For me. (*Stopping.*) Stand off till I get a good look at you. (*Putting* RUTH *at arm's length.*) You are so beautiful. You always were the beautiful one.

AILEEN. Thanks very much.

DOPHIE. But you cut off all your lovely long hair.

MA. Sure Mammy Ruth hasn't had long hair since she made her First Holy Communion.

DOPHIE. And would you look at her in trousers.

RUTH (*a little strained*). You're looking very well today too, Nana. (*Tucking in her label at the back.*) I've a present for you. From America.

She hands her her box.

DOPHIE. From America? Oh Lordy. For me? (*Nervously handing it back.*) You open it. From America.

RUTH *takes it and opens it. It is a long white embroidered night-gown.*

RUTH. I made it myself Nana.

Slowly DOPHIE *takes it in her hands. She feels the material, carefully examines its weight, the stitching, the embroidery. She smells it. She speaks purposefully – as if delivering a verdict.*

DOPHIE. Fine cloth. Good and tight. A good weight to it too. The girls on the cutting-room floor would thank you for that. And a good finish. I was always one for a good finish. That was my hall-mark, you know.

MA. You've a grand memory when it serves you Mammy. You haven't set foot inside a shirt factory in decades, but you can't remember where you left your teeth this morning.

RUTH (*proudly*). And look Dophie. I never forgot.

She points out the slipped stitches to DOPHIE. DOPHIE *studies it and smiles.*

DOPHIE. Oh look! (*Pause.*) You missed a couple of stitches there.

The wind goes out of RUTH.

DOPHIE. Look.

RUTH. I see it.

DOPHIE. Shame. It's nearly perfect otherwise. (*Handing it back.*) If you lift them carefully you could probably still get it past the examiners. With a bit of luck.

RUTH. Hang on to it for now Dophie. It's for you. It's a present for you.

DOPHIE *looks confused.*

RUTH. Remember? I made it for you. Well, I designed it. I had one of the girls at the factory make it up.

DOPHIE. I hope she didn't get caught. Not on my account. You could get some poor girl into a lot of trouble for that sort of carry on.

RUTH. Don't you worry about that. She had full permission.

DOPHIE. Well they must be very nice men over there then. They wouldn't let you do that sort of thing here, that's for sure.

RUTH. What men?

DOPHIE. The Big Bosses.

RUTH. The buck stops here, Dophie. I *am* the Big Boss. Me and Mabs McGinty. It's our factory. We own it.

MA. Remember we took you out and showed you where the new one's at? Out beside Roaring Meg's Pub?

DOPHIE (*mulling it over*). Two girls? Is that how they do things in America?

RUTH. It's how *I* do things.

Beat.

DOPHIE. Yes. I'm so glad. Owns a factory in America! Oh! So glad it all came good in the end Catherine. So glad.

RUTH. Ruth, Dophie.

DOPHIE. I can rest easy in myself now. Thank-you.

She takes back the night gown and starts to strip down to her drawers and vest.

MA. Spare us Mammy, please. Could you not do that upstairs?

Dismissively DOPHIE hands MA her dress.

DOPHIE. Thank you, Miss.

MA (*taking it*). Och don't mind me.

DOPHIE *pulls the gown on over her head, getting lost in the process, affording them all a giggle. Eventually she gets her head through and smooths the gown down over herself and stands all smiles like a little girl.*

AILEEN. You can keep that for your trousseau, Nana.

MA. Shroud more like.

AILEEN. Mammy.

Cradling the gown to herself, she waltzes a moment, humming Tommy Dorsey's Polka Dots and Moonbeams, and looking for her exit.

DOPHIE. I knew you were on your way Catherine. I'll rest now.

MA (*pointing her towards the stairs*). That way.

DOPHIE (*cross*). I know that, you.

RUTH. Dophie, it's Ruth.

DOPHIE (*stopping at* MA). Look at the state of you. You're soaking wet. And us with company in. Do something with yourself would you? (*Dancing off.*)

Exit DOPHIE.

Beat.

RUTH. Did she know me?

MA. Course she did, she was delighted to see you. Sure weren't you always her wee pet? Hers and your father's.

RUTH *smiles.*

RUTH. Who's Catherine?

MA. God only knows. A name she pulled out of a hat. Don't let it worry you love, at least you've got a name. I'm just the wee woman who does.

RUTH *sits down at the table.*

I don't know does she even remember my name. What's wrong?

RUTH. Nothing. I'm just a bit confused.

MA. Well you'll fit right in then. I'm sorry love. I would have given you more warning but you didn't give us much – (*She backs off.*) Don't fret yourself. She has her good days too you know. It comes over her in tides. And you certainly brought the best out in her – I haven't been able to put a smile on that face for months.

AILEEN. Not unless you're feeding it Bon-bons.

MA. And she sure as hell hasn't *taken* anything off anyone in as long as I can remember. Not off me anyway.

AILEEN. Bon-bons.

MA. Not off me. She has my heart broken. (*Shouting up the stairs.*) Mammy do you want this dress? Mammy?! (*No answer.*) Oh, I may go up and see to her. (*As it dawns.*) Was that you up with her in the middle of the night then?

RUTH. Well I was up with Dophie. I'm not so sure now *who* Dophie was up with.

MA. Poor Mammy. Getting herself all dolled up and no wee trip for her. She loves an outing.

AILEEN. We'll sit her in the van later and run the engine. She's just as happy with that.

Exit MA.

Welcome home.

MA (*offstage*). Sixty quid. Honest to God.

RUTH. Jesus. You'd think I'd spent the family fortune. She's as tight.

AILEEN. She's careful. There's a difference.

RUTH. She's tight.

AILEEN. Don't start Ruth.

RUTH. Sorry. She's just got me wound up. She's a bit wound up herself, isn't she?

AILEEN. All the excitement of you coming home, believe it or not. She even got her hair done. Tell her it looks nice or something would you?

RUTH. She looks exhausted.

AILEEN. That's how she shows her devotion. She's worried. (*Pause.*) She thinks he must have been hitting you. (*Pause.*) Ruth?

No reply.

Are you okay?

RUTH (*looking round the room*). I just feel a bit strange, that's all. All the changes and everything.

AILEEN. No I mean –

RUTH. I know what you mean.

Beat.

AILEEN. Ok. Moving swiftly on, what's the plan now then, now that you're here?

RUTH. Exactly the same as it always was. My business and my life *here*. Sure I only went in the first place so I could come back. All I *could* do since tight-arse wouldn't give me a lending hand.

AILEEN. Couldn't.

RUTH. What-ever. And I've done it. It only took for bloody ever, but I've done it. Home in glory. Great, isn't it?

AILEEN. It is Ruth.

RUTH. What?

AILEEN. Nothing. It *is* great. It just seems a bit strange that you have exactly the same goals that you did when you were seventeen. I mean did the goal-posts not shift *at all* in between?

RUTH. Call me focused.

AILEEN. Blinkered more like. Ruth you can't just pick up from seventeen again and pretend as if nothing happened in between. There's ones in Gransha for less.

RUTH. That is so not what I'm doing. My life is here. I'm just a wee Derry girl at heart.

AILEEN. Maybe. But the goal posts must have shifted for a while anyway with Matt? Well I think it's safe to assume he's not hitting you, not the Matt I ever met anyway, nearly as nice as Daddy, however you wangled that for yourself.

Beat.

Jesus Christ Ruth I can't believe you packed all that in for *this*. What the hell happened you?

RUTH. Would you let up?! I don't *know* Aileen! I wish to fuck I did. Look, me and you grew up on red sauce and brown sauce and Doherty's mince, right? And then for me it was suddenly all guacamole and dips and lox and . . . aghhh . . . I don't *know* Aileen. Nothing in my life was *me* anymore. I felt totally . . . disconnected. Jesus, part of me still can't believe what I've done. I can't picture my life without him. . . but I just couldn't picture myself living there either.

AILEEN. But you were living there.

RUTH. I know. But I never intended to be.

AILEEN. Well if it was all so bad Ruth, why did you leave it till now? You've been planning this wedding all year and then you bail with less than six weeks to go.

RUTH. It wasn't *just* a wedding Aileen, it was the point of no return! Ha! It used to be the emigrant's *wake* that marked that. Lovely imagery. Wedding, wake, wake, wedding. Emigrant, immigrant, immigrant, emigrant – swap a whole world for one little vowel. And then there was Mabs going home with Maiden City – all I ever worked for. None of me seemed to be in the right place at the right time. Ruth Sweeney, Missing In Action. Ha! Like the boys at the dinosaur mall.

AILEEN. You wouldn't be human Ruth if you weren't scared.

RUTH. Scared? There were days I couldn't *move*. And then days I just went around like a Stepford fiancée with a big Xanex-induced smile –

AILEEN. Ruth, are you sure this isn't just pre-wedding nerves?

RUTH. For God's sake Aileen! This has nothing to do with the 'I do' bit – the 'I take you as my lawfully wedded husband' part! I *really* wanted that. Believe me. It was all the rest – the unwritten 'I also take your guacamole and your zucchinis and your – *sink disposal units!!!*' The 'I agree to pull a big switch in my head and somehow just forget about *home*' and have children with American accents who will call me Mom and go to first grade and high school and wear bobby socks and bobby pins and always a feeling of what if? What if I'd gone back? What if I'd never left? What would the Irish me be doing now? What would my Irish children be like? And my Irish husband? And what would – what – ah what the fuck does Socrates know about electricity anyway?!

AILEEN. Are you still taking the tablets?

RUTH. Fuck off.

AILEEN. You'll have regrets both ways Ruth.

RUTH. At last she grasps it. (*Pause.*) I'm doing the right thing. I know I am. Surely it's better to deal with the what-ifs now than be stuck with the if-onlys later?

Beat.

AILEEN. But I thought you were always dying to have weans?

RUTH. My 'quickenings'? (*They share a smile.*) I am. Matt wanted a baseball team. (*Pause.*) I really wish I could have obliged.

AILEEN. Maybe you'll get a GAA team instead.

RUTH (*Pause.*) You're lucky Aileen, you never had this curve-ball thrown at you. I wish I'd never had to leave. Do you remember *Ruth's Glad Rags*? All my plans for that? (*Laughing.*) Desperate name, isn't it? Ah well, it never got beyond its name anyway and that's a crying fucking shame because I could have pulled it off in a heart-beat. With a bit of support. You got to steer a straight course. Look at you, on your way to a house and a husband and your own business up and thriving in the town. Isn't it great? I'm delighted for you. All I ever wanted. So straight-forward.

The phone rings.

AILEEN. Aye, wee buns. (*She picks up.*) Derry 71262608. . . Pardon? . . . Eh? (*She looks confused.*) Hang on a minute. (*Handing the phone to* RUTH.) It's for you. I think. (*Taking the piss.*) Who's *Root Schveeney?*

RUTH. We're exhibiting at the Trade Fair in Frankfurt. (*Into the phone.*) Hallo?

DOPHIE *enters, still in the nightie. Excited.*

RUTH. Oh, hallo, am – Do you speak English? . . . *Bitte?*

DOPHIE (*to* RUTH). The savage loves his native shore!

RUTH (*hand over phone*). Eh?

AILEEN *is pulling on her jacket.*

(*Pulled back to the phone.*) Oh sorry. Look I don't understand you. Marcus Riecke was supposed to be ringing me –

DOPHIE. Cigars and gasoline!

RUTH. What? (*To* AILEEN.) Where are you going? Oh, (*back to phone.*) Marcus? Tut. Is Marcus Riecke there bitte? (*Hand over phone again.*) Aileen?

DOPHIE. And Little Women!

RUTH (*to* DOPHIE). Sssh. (*To* AILEEN, *who is slipping out the back door with a big smile and a wave.*) Give us a hand with this, would you?

AILEEN. You just said you were homesick, well there it is on a plate for you. I'm away out for a fag.

RUTH. You don't still have to –

AILEEN. I don't 'have to' anything Ruth.

Exit AILEEN.

RUTH (*abruptly into phone*). Look I need to speak to Marcus
    Riecke please.

DOPHIE. Cigars and gasoline and *still* you couldn't stay away!

RUTH. Never mind love. I'll try myself later.

She hangs up. DOPHIE *gives the material in* RUTH's
trousers a perfunctory feel.

DOPHIE. Sure you only went away so you could get wearing
    those things.

RUTH. In a way.

DOPHIE. The Big Boss, eh?

RUTH. That would be me.

DOPHIE. I always kept my faith in you, Catherine.

RUTH. Dophie, my name is Ruth.

DOPHIE. Nobody more so than me. I promise. (*Pause.*) Have a
    Bon-bon.

RUTH. No thanks. Really.

DOPHIE. I wish you would. Somebody has to eat the things.
    She keeps on buying them – I have to keep on eating them.
    She can be very 'um-hum' that woman, when she wants to
    be.

RUTH. Can't she just? (*Taking a sweet.*) Go on then.

DOPHIE. Look at you. Like a Hollywood ending. I have
    something to puff myself up about now.

RUTH (*touched*). Thank you.

DOPHIE. I always knew it. Beautiful creature. My light.

MA (*shouting from up the stairs*). Mammy!

DOPHIE (*immediately distressed*). Oh no! (*She can't get out of
    the room.*) I'm sorry Catherine! I *wanted* to go down and
    wave to you but they wouldn't let me!

MA (*off-stage*). Mammy!!

DOPHIE. They made me stay home and do my lessons –

MA (*off-stage*). Mammy!

DOPHIE. All on your own watching the water widen from the
    dock's edge. No-one to wave you off –

RUTH. What?

MA (*off-stage*). Do I have to come down those stairs?

DOPHIE. I should have waved! Given you my blessing. I'm sorry!

MA (*off-stage*). *Mammy!!!*

DOPHIE. *WHAT?!*

MA (*off-stage*). Have you brushed your teeth?

DOPHIE (*hushed*). Catherine, she's stolen all the money.

RUTH. Who has?

DOPHIE. I brushed them!! I brushed them!!

MA (*off-stage*). Your tooth brush is bone dry Mammy.

DOPHIE. That woman leaves it on the radiator.

RUTH. Mammy?

DOPHIE. That's *our* money! Our hard money. I know where it came from and you know where it came from.

RUTH. Dophie, Mammy is not taking your money. That's ridiculous.

Enter MA.

MA. Right. Come on you. Wash. (*Trying to herd her up the stairs.*) Come on now. It'll hardly kill you.

DOPHIE *wants to stay with* RUTH.

You'd think I was an ogre or something.

RUTH. Go on Nana. I'll still be here.

DOPHIE (*gingerly side-stepping* MA *on her way upstairs*). Mind the material.

MA. You can put it back on again you know. Just so long as you wash.

Exit DOPHIE.

(*Lifting a laundry basket and heading to the back door.*) That day's turning on us. (*Up the stairs.*) And wee-wees while you're up there!

DOPHIE (*off-stage*). I don't have to go.

MA. Course you do. You can't take it with you.

A gush of water is heard from upstairs.

Mammy!! Turn off those taps this instant! Do you HEAR me?!

DOPHIE (*off-stage*). It helps me to go!

MA (*marching to the bottom of the stairs*). I'm *warning* you! God help you if I have to come *up* the stairs now!

RUTH. You go on Mammy. I'll see to her.

Pause.

MA. Just make sure I don't need oars to get back in.

Exit MA.

RUTH. Turn them off Dophie. You can come back down. She's gone.

The sound of the water running stops. Enter DOPHIE, the front of her night-gown all wet.

I guess that's you washed then. Do you want to move into the sitting room with me?

DOPHIE. We can't. She has it reserved.

RUTH. For what?

DOPHIE. For special. We have to stay here. I'm hungry. I never got any breakfast you know.

RUTH. Oh. Am, dinner's a bit of a way off. But not too long.

DOPHIE. Could I have an egg-in-a-cup?

RUTH. What? Oh, yes, of course.

RUTH goes about boiling an egg.

DOPHIE. Not runny please.

Enter AILEEN with a lit butt.

AILEEN. Thanks for the warning.

She strides across the stage and exits through the living room.

DOPHIE (*lighting up*). Egg in a cup for Saturday lunch waiting for our hair to dry!

RUTH. Who?

DOPHIE. And you in your bright red uniform. I loved you in that. The only bit of colour in the whole house. Beautiful.

RUTH's confusion gives way to curiosity and she sits down to listen.

DOPHIE. I was scared of the buttons though, wasn't I? I could see myself upside-down in them. You showed me not to be scared because I was upside-down in the spoons too. But I never really saw how that helped any.

RUTH laughs.

RUTH. What else do you remember Dophie?

DOPHIE. And your bright red lipstick to match! The one you said Rita Hayworth wore. I bet she didn't have to sneak it on in a back-lane though. And then I'd be walking behind Rita Hayworth past all the queue and everybody looking at us because we were obviously people of some import. Remember? (RUTH *nods*.) Right in through the slidey doors holding your hand and never had to pay. We loved it in there didn't we?

RUTH. I can see that *you* did.

DOPHIE. Oh yes. And I never got scared on my own in the dark because I knew you were right at the back, looking out for me, with your torch.

RUTH. Ah.

DOPHIE. And we saw *everything* didn't we? For free! Every film there ever was! Much better than when you worked on the buses and all we got was free rides to all sorts of places you wouldn't want to go to anyway. You used to say the ride home was the worst. After Francis. But that anything was better than the factories. 'Over my dead body!' 'Over my dead body!' (DOPHIE *is starting to get upset*.) 'Over my dead body.'

RUTH. It's all right, Dophie, it's all right –

DOPHIE (*calming*). Yes. You're here with me now. Aren't you Catherine?

RUTH. Yes. I'm here.

DOPHIE. Yes. And you made a fine fist of the factories after all. Didn't you?

RUTH. I guess I did. (*Pause.*) And what then Dophie?

DOPHIE (*her mood changing*). And then after we saw the film, you'd tell me you were going to run away to Hollywood and marry Cary Grant!

RUTH. A girl could do worse –

DOPHIE. And I'd lie awake at night listening in case you did. I was so scared you'd go. And leave me. So scared. So then you said I could go too and marry Mickey Rooney. But that made me cry even more. But then I said I would go when I saw *Little Women*. All those sisters! But you had to promise me we wouldn't see Mickey Rooney there. (*Bitter.*) It's a hard thing to do, you know. For a little girl.

RUTH. What is?

DOPHIE. Replace a dead brother.

RUTH. What?

DOPHIE. All by myself. After you left. Went without me.

Pause.

RUTH. I'm sorry, Dophie.

DOPHIE. I fair soaked my pillow to get going after you.

DOPHIE *is agitated – up and pacing.*

All that water now must be getting back into my head when I lie down on it. (*Holding her head.*) I feel like it's going to burst. Sometimes I think all of the Atlantic must be in there by now. Too much pressure.

She heads for the taps. RUTH *guides her back to the table.* DOPHIE *blocks her ears and starts rocking her head.*

RUTH (*alarmed*). What's wrong Dophie? Dophie?

DOPHIE (*snapping to*). He was well-named, wasn't he?

RUTH. Who was?

DOPHIE. That's something I always thought. Did you too? 'Free!' Christened and buried all in the one winter. Poor mite.

RUTH. Who Dophie?

DOPHIE. Little Baby Francis. That's what Francis means isn't it? Free!

RUTH. Why? What happened to him? (*Catching herself.*) Remind me.

DOPHIE. You never wanted to remember did you? (*Slowly recalling.*) We were playing in the room. Film Stars. You were in charge of us. And we had Mammy's big feathers from her wedding hat and we were doing Esther Williams, swimming and diving all afternoon on the big bed. Remember?

RUTH *nods her on. Beat.*

And Little Baby Francis fast asleep on it. We forgot. He was so little. Not a peep out of him to warn us –

RUTH. Oh my God, Dophie.

DOPHIE. Remember?

RUTH *is shocked. She nods.*

And you supposed to be minding him. Poor little Baby Francis. And poor Mother – finding him like that all squashed between the bed and the wall. No sound. No sound anymore. Just the sound of you peeing yourself all over the lino. When they pulled the bed back.

Beat.

She left you no room in the house after that. I suppose you had to go.

RUTH. I suppose.

DOPHIE. As soon as you could get a wherewithal.

Beat.

I hated you for leaving me.

RUTH. I'm sorry Dophie.

DOPHIE. And you were free then too. But not me. I had to stay. With that.

Beat.

RUTH (*hearing something*). That's Mammy back.

DOPHIE *panics.*

You don't have to go. Sit and have your egg.

A moment of confusion, and DOPHIE *beats a hasty retreat. Enter* MA *with her washing from the line and starts folding it into the hot-cupboard.*

MA. That cold is marrow-deep. Either I'm going to rot or I'm going to rust this summer, I can't decide which. Is this your egg?

RUTH. It's for Dophie. She says she'd no breakfast.

MA. And she tells the whole street I lock her in her room and only let her out to do the house-work. Whatever Happened to Baby Dophie?

Re-enter AILEEN – *she goes to the dinner preparations again.*

AILEEN. She'd a feed of porridge and scones Ruth. She forgets.

RUTH. And she says you've spent all her money.

MA (*laughing*). Did you not see the yacht out the back?

RUTH. What does the doctor say about her?

MA. Sure what can he say? She's been going like this for the past sixteen or seventeen years – I'm sure if he had a miracle cure, he'd have said something about it by now.

AILEEN. She has you for Kitty. She had me for Big Josephine all last week.

RUTH. Who's Kitty?

MA. Of course, Kitty. The sister.

RUTH (*as it comes together*). Catherine.

MA. I forgot about her.

RUTH. How could you forget about her sister?

MA. I never even knew there *was* a sister till after she was dead.

RUTH. Really?

MA. Oh aye. Totally taboo subject with Mammy. Ditsy Kitsy and her GI Joe. I don't know how come she's all blather about her now for. You must look like her or something.

AILEEN. That or you both went off to America.

RUTH (*excited*). Catherine went to America?

AILEEN. Well she married a GI didn't she?

MA. Something like that.

RUTH. At least she got her Cary Grant.

MA (*making a dig*). And there I guess the parallel ends.

    Beat – RUTH *lets it go.*

RUTH. Tell us more. It must have been some scandal.

MA. I'm sure it was. (*Shelling the egg for egg-in-a-cup.*) It's a good job she doesn't like them runny. You could take somebody's eye out with this. Seemingly the oul Da hit the roof altogether. 'Good enough for a Bogside trollop maybe, but not for a McDaid.' And the McDaids only one generation out of the Bog, but that was another thing you never talked about. He was one snob. A right dour oul git altogether.

RUTH. It must have been a hard house for them to grow up in.

MA. I'd say Catherine just wanted to grab her first ticket out of there. They cut her off then. Just went on as if she was dead. I suppose she was to all intents and purposes.

RUTH. But not Dophie?

MA. Ha! According to Daddy, she was the worst of the lot of them. Vicious.

RUTH. Really? Dophie?

MA. One and the same. Never forgave her.

RUTH. Never?

MA. Never ever. Never broke breath with her again.

Beat.

RUTH. And what about Francis?

MA. Who?

RUTH. The brother. Didn't they have a little brother Francis?

MA. No. No, there was no brother. Just the two of them. What made you think that?

A knock on the back-door as it opens. MAB *lets herself in. She is a flurry of chat and duty-free bags and coats and cigarettes. Big and ebullient, expensively dressed, but couldn't really be bothered to carry it.*

MAB (*all grins*). Well? How's the girls? How's the form?

ALL THREE. Mab!!!

MAB (*to* RUTH). You made it then? You head-the-ball. Welcome home. (*Mouths.*) Later. Och Dolores! (*Hugging* MA.) Great to see you again. You look brilliant so you do. Great hair-do. (MA *beams.*) C'mere, I've been meaning to take a wee scoot over all week but my life's a bedlam. I'm up to me oxters in weans and work. Here, have youse an ashtray? (MA *hands her one.*) Jesus Aileen I'd hardly recognise you. Well what about you you skinny bitch? (*Hugging her.*) I'd be afeard of snapping you. (*Taking off her coat.*) I'm melted so I am. No harm to you Ruth, but you're wrecked looking. That journey's desperate isn't it? My ankles are *still* swollen. Ah well, more of me to love. And I'll never have to do it again. Thank God. (*Lighting up and looking at* RUTH.) Nor you either, eh? Now. (*Offering a cigarette to a mortified* AILEEN.) It's great to be back isn't it? There's a bottle for you Dolores in one of them bags. (*Swanky.*) Bourbon. (*She brings out another bottle.*) And a bottle of Gordon's. You couldn't forget the Gordon's. Do you see if I ever have another son, I'm going to *call* him Gordon. (*Lifting up the Battenberg – to* MA.) You rolling out the red carpet?

RUTH. Mab, do us a favour. Breathe.

MAB. I know, what am I like? I only shut up to drag. Something smells good.

MA. Stay and eat with us Mab, I'd love that. A crowded table again. You will won't you? (*Lifting the bottle of Bourbon.*) God bless you child, knickers are all very well, but there's not much drinking in them.

RUTH. Well thank-you very much.

MAB. No. But you might get a bit of action in them, eh Dolores?

MA (*laughing*). And I thought youse were a classy outfit.

MAB. We are. 'Maiden City – Trousseau Treasures. The Very best of Irish Linen and Lace Couture.' The Yanks love that. (*She picks up* MA*'s knickers.*) Get their arses right down into the oul sod. You could sell them anything.

RUTH. *You* could sell them anything.

MAB. If it's Irish. They'd frame a crisp if you told them the spud came from the same county as their great-great-grandfather.

MA (*laughing*). You haven't lost your accent any Mab. That's for sure.

MAB. God forbid.

MA. Not like this one.

RUTH. I said garbage.

MAB. Very dangerous.

AILEEN. And trash.

MAB. Oooh. Sure you're great over there. More Yank than the Yankies.

RUTH. Tools of survival. And look who's talking. More Paddy than the Paddies.

MAB. My tools. (*To* MA.) I was always having to put her on the phone for me. They never knew what I was banging on about half the time. 'I'm sorry Ma'am, unfortunately we have no Spanish-speaking personnel in the office at present.' Spanish, like. I ask you. Here I get on the phone and they just want to speak to the man. C'mere, did you see last week's Derry Journal?

MA (*setting a place for* MAB). I did. One of the neighbours showed it to me.

AILEEN. Ha!!!

MA *shoots her daggers.*

MAB. Great wee spread wasn't it?

RUTH. What? *Local Lasses Done Good?*

MAB. Desperate picture of you in it. We'll have to get you a copy for the craic.

AILEEN (*getting a copy from the sideboard*). Sure we have it here.

RUTH. You kept it Mammy?

AILEEN. Kept it? Who do you think put it in? It's in there with all your feis medals and embroidery samplers and everything else in the 'shrine to Ruthie.'

RUTH (*all delighted*). Is that right Mammy?

MA. Don't be daft. Aileen that's just rubbish piling up. Those drawers need a good redding out. How's your Mother keeping Mab?

RUTH *deflates.* AILEEN *hands her the paper.*

MAB. In her element. She's bumming her load all over town any chance she can get. 'What our Mab hasn't done and what our Mab can't show yees all isn't worth the knowing.' She'd sicken you.

AILEEN. Like someone else's mother I know.

MA. Who?

AILEEN. Sure you have the neighbours poisoned.

MA (*dryly*). Um hum.

MAB. She has those wee fellas of mine spoilt rotten, so she has. You want to hear them. They're only back a wet week and they're already sticking 'hi' and 'but' and 'you know lick' on the end of everything. Wee shites. Running riot all over the place. We're living heads and thraws over there. It's doing my Martin's nut in. God love him, he wasn't in the door two minutes before he had the Property pages out. And I think me Da's afraid to come home altogether. He's volunteered to go over to me Auntie Agnes till we get sorted and only come home for his dinner. Good of him, wasn't it? (*Laughing.*) I don't think me Ma would notice the difference.

MA (*laughing*). You'd think one of these big heifers of mine would get around to producing me a grandchild some time soon. I can't seem to get them shifted at all. (*Realising.*)

AILEEN. Nice one Ma.

All eyes to RUTH, *still reading the paper.*

RUTH (*a veiled smile*). Typical of you Mammy. Tell the world asunder how brilliant I am, but God forbid you told me yourself.

MAB. Afraid of you getting a swollen head.

RUTH. Not likely, in this place. And what's this? A hundred workers under us? Quite the embellishment.

MAB. Sure that's what Mammies are supposed to do.

RUTH (*quoting*). And 'Maiden City already employs over five hundred workers in their mother plant in the US-'. News to me. Mammy we've never had more than three hundred, even in our peak times, and you know it. Is that not good enough for you? And could you have *found* a worse-looking photograph?

MA. I better go and look in on the Mammy. She's suspiciously quiet too long me thinks. That's just the Journal getting it all wrong, Ruth. As usual.

Exit MA.

MAB (*as soon as* MA *is gone*). Ruth, are you all right? Jesus, how's Dolores taking it? I didn't know what I was going to find here the day at all. Ruth?

AILEEN. Dolores will be just fine.

MAB. And Matt is in bits. I rang to see how he was – (RUTH *eyeballs her*.) well I wasn't getting anything out of you. According to his Da he hasn't been into work all week and he's put the house on the market.

RUTH. Already?

MAB. Must have been some bust-up. What happened youse?

MAB waits in vain to be filled in. She looks from one sister to the other.

MAB. Closing rank on me then?

She lights another cigarette and continues on.

I know how you felt about staying Ruth. But did youse have to split up? Surely he could be here now too.

RUTH. I never asked him.

MAB. That's what I mean.

RUTH. To leave his family and his business?

MAB. Why not? You did it.

RUTH. Exactly. (*Pause.*) I sounded him out plenty Mab – he didn't want me to ask him. I know he didn't. Anyway what would it solve? We'd just have been having all the same problems, only in reverse.

AILEEN. But –

RUTH. Can we just leave it there?

Beat.

MAB. What's all your craic then Aileen, since I saw you last? Still Fleet-Footing it?

AILEEN. Flat-footing it more like. We had to ditch two vans last month. Unfortunately that's half the 'fleet.'

RUTH. Why?

AILEEN. No business. Whatever's going on in the rest of the country, there's not much movement up this way yet. In or out. Doesn't bode well for a transport company, does it?

RUTH. You never said Aileen.

AILEEN. You never asked Ruth.

MAB. Put in to us. We'll be moving a lot of stock around the country after the launch. (*Rubbing her hands.*) There'll be buyers scurrying in the length and breadth of the land.

AILEEN. My bid is already in Mab. And a very competitive one at that I'll have you know. No nepotism for this girl.

MAB. Ach it's yours. (*Distracted – listening to something in the distance.*) Is that the Angelus? I've to take me pill. (*She starts rooting through her handbag.*)

RUTH. Why didn't you sink in the money I've been sending you? That's what it's for. Or have more, if you want. You might as well since the Ma won't have any truck with it. Pardon the pun.

AILEEN. Neil's a stubborn thick. Sees it as a handout. Don't worry Ruth – it's all gone on a down-payment. Bricks and mortar.

MAB. Who's this Neil?

RUTH. Neil McGettigan. Who do you think?

MAB. Baps McGettigan! Is that still going strong? In bed and in business with him now? Look at the redner on her! Should I be buying a hat then?

AILEEN. You can hang on to your money a while yet Mab.

MAB. Oh really? You going to be shacking up? Dolores can't be too happy about that.

AILEEN. Dolores is learning to live with it. As am I.

MAB. That must've taken some doing.

RUTH. I know Aileen, you shouldn't let her –

AILEEN. I don't 'let her' anything Ruth. In the door five minutes and she thinks she knows all about it.

RUTH. I'm only saying.

AILEEN. I know what you're only saying.

MAB. You must be going with him ten years.

AILEEN. Aye. Almost.

MAB. God, wee Bapser was still booting about on his BMX last time I saw him. So when do we get to meet him?

AILEEN. I'll see if I can pencil you in. I feel like I'm having a relationship with a one-way cab radio at the minute. We're all over the shop.

MAB. But we'll see him at the launch? (*Still rooting.*) Shit. I've forgot the bloody things again.

AILEEN. Should I be buying little booties then Mab?

MAB. Very funny. (*Closing her bag.*) I'm only conning myself I'm taking the bloody yokes anyway. If it keeps my Martin happy –

Enter MA.

MA. She'll be down in a minute. I think all the voices must be scaring her. (*Smelling the dinner.*) Mmmmm.

MAB (*to* RUTH). I see your Charlie's Angels poster is gone.

RUTH. I know. Is *nothing* sacred?

AILEEN. I did my best to try and save it.

MAB *strikes up the theme tune. All laughing, they strike the pose.*

RUTH. I loved playing that. It's funny how all our memories of childhood are actually memories of America.

AILEEN (*going to pull the only other chair left over to the table*). Are we using Daddy's chair Mammy?

MA. Well none of us could fill it, but one of us might as well sit in it.

MAB. He was hardly *that* fat Dolores.

Beat.

MA. That's not what I meant Mab. Not what I meant at all.

MAB *is momentarily silenced.* MA *produces the bottle of champagne from the fridge.*

RUTH. Champagne? La-di-da.

AILEEN. Exactly what I said. And *Asti Spumante* too if you don't mind.

RUTH. Are we celebrating Mammy?

MA. Are we Ruth?

Enter DOPHIE. *She is still wearing the night-gown.*

MAB. Would you look at this vision coming? How are you Mrs Carlin?

No answer.

Well you look lovely so you do. (*To* RUTH.) Is that one of ours?

RUTH. Su Ling ran it up for me.

MAB. You could get a job modelling for us couldn't you Mrs Carlin?

DOPHIE. Yes.

MA. We'll never get her out of it again. Will we Mammy?

DOPHIE. Please may I leave the table?

MA. Stay with us. Sure you just sat down. You remember Mab, don't you? Mab is just back from America too.

DOPHIE. From America.

MA. Ruth's school friend. The pair of them went off together. Mind?

DOPHIE *nods slowly and sits down opposite* RUTH *studying her intently.* MA *is clucking around like a mother hen.* AILEEN *takes a seat. No-one sits in the Da's chair.*

You do the honours then Aileen.

AILEEN, *her bum barely in the chair, gets up to crack the champagne.*

AILEEN. Just the wee dog –

RUTH. – we always had. Swap you?

AILEEN. I don't know what you think I have that you'd want. Here she goes!

The champagne pops. They all cheer and scoop their glasses under.

AILEEN. Well, welcome home girls! To Maiden City *in* the Maiden City! To your success!

MAB. And much much more of it!

MA. I hope so.

MAB. Ah Dolores, don't worry yourself. You'll be getting a Porsche for Christmas!

MA. I hope so. No! Sure what would I be doing with a Porsche? No, I just hope youse know what you're doing that's all.

RUTH. Flatten our bubbles why don't you?

MA. I'm just worried – how you're going to manage a business there and a business here with both of you in Derry now is beyond me Ruth.

RUTH. Anyone would think you didn't want me home.

MA. Well it made sense to me before with you holding the fort over there, but no-one's in any great rush to point out to me how it's all going to work now, are they?

Everyone stands around awkwardly with their glasses raised.

RUTH. Look it's sorted. We both work from here and the American one's being franchised. They do all the work and we make all the money. No-risk-sure-fire. We have it sewn up.

DOPHIE *laughs. They all look at her in surprise. Then they get the joke.*

MA. Dear God. The wit. I've come out the foul end of a sure-fire-no-risk business venture before Ruth, don't forget. And the toll wasn't worth it, believe you me.

RUTH. That was different. Daddy opened up a second bread shop just when the supermarkets were starting to get a hold of the town –

MA. I still couldn't buy a loaf of bread out of one of them. (*To* AILEEN.) I hate it when you bring it into the house –

DOPHIE. I hate it too.

MA. And surely Ruth you'd more than work to keep you there?

RUTH. Or maybe Mammy I'd more to bring me home.

MA. But you can design from anywhere, can't you, push of a button? I thought that was all the fuss about computers these days. Seems to me you could have had your cake *and* the icing –

RUTH (*finally snapping*). Jesus Christ sorry to be putting you out Mammy. I didn't realise when you put me out the door you weren't letting me back in again.

MA. I hardly 'put you out the door' Ruth.

RUTH. No just held it open for me.

DOPHIE (*pointing at* MAB). I remember you. You were the one with the nits.

MA. Mammy! What brought that on?

DOPHIE. I remember things.

MAB. Jesus she's right. Mind? Me Ma and Da had gone to Rome to see the Pope and by the time she got back I'd given them to half our estate. The head was leppin' off me. You've some memory Mrs Carlin.

MA. Ha.

MAB (*feigning bashfulness*). Dear, I'm as affronted so I am.

DOPHIE. I remember. (*Slowly.*) And then you went to America. (*Looking at* RUTH.) And then you went to America.

DOPHIE *rises to go.*

MA. Mammy sit, please. I want you to stay with us.

She presses DOPHIE *who sits and starts to smooth down the tablecloth again.*

Do you see this tablecloth Mab? Mammy made this, didn't you Mammy? (*No reply.*) Out of flax grown on her great Aunt Josephine's farm that was spun and woven by her daughter Eva, my great aunt. And Mammy hemmed it and did all that lovely open embroidery work, isn't that right, Mammy?

DOPHIE. Remnants.

MA (*laughing*). Us or the tablecloth? (*No reply.*) I remember her at it for months. And didn't I help you? So I did. I did a wee bit of the hemming on that corner there. (AILEEN*'s corner.*) That's my first bit of needlework ever. I think I was about six at the time.

AILEEN (*turning the cloth over*). It looks like the handiwork of a six-year-old all right. No offence Ma, but it's falling apart.

RUTH. Let me see that. (*She examines it.*) That's deliberate. That's Dophie's three slipped stitches!

MA. Let me see. I don't know about that Ruth.

RUTH. It *is*.

MA. Is it Mammy?

DOPHIE. You hemmed by the rose-buds. (*The other corner*).

MA (*checking*). She's right. You remember that?

RUTH. Do you remember Nana?

MA. I'll have to fix that.

RUTH. No don't!

AILEEN. Why? In case we all get struck down?

RUTH. It *is* the slipped stitches, isn't it Dophie? (DOPHIE *doesn't respond*.) Jesus I hope so. Otherwise I just spent the last fifteen years building up a whole wee tradition for myself based on nothing. Dishing up faulty merchandise to the high-society ladies of Philadelphia for no good reason. I slipped the last three stitches on everything – for you Nana. Don't fix it.

DOPHIE. You could have done that here.

MA. And do you see in that corner there Mab beside you? That dirty big stain? Adding to its intrinsic value? That's where our Ruth knocked over a whole glass of red wine about ten Christmases ago.

RUTH. And is kilt apologising for it ever since. Pity it couldn't have been something a bit more creative. But then that's what I'm doing now isn't it? And I made a good fist of it, didn't I, Nana?

MA. Just you remember this Ruth, nothing you have done, you did by yourself. You've a lot of people on down your line to thank for your achievements. Ones that worked harder than you, and got nothing for their pains, but paved your way.

The wind is taken out of RUTH.

(*Running her hand over the stain*.) Anyway, that stain's there for all time now. And for that reason I'm rather partial to it. So there's five people and five generations sitting around this table with us now. And every time this cloth comes out, I think of every one of them – you. (*Catching herself on*.) But you can pass that one there (MAB.) an ashtray before she adds a great big fag burn as her own personal contribution.

MAB. Oh Jesus. Sorry. That would be my hallmark all right. It's certainly a fine piece of work, Dolores.

MA. Not particularly. But I'd save it in a fire. (*Getting up to put the finishing touches on the dinner*.) Warm five plates for us Aileen. Just run them under the hot tap.

MAB (*getting up*). None for me Dolores. Honestly. I need to be getting back. I told them at home I was only taking a wee scoot.

MA (*bringing a huge leg of lamb to the table*). Not at all, you're more than welcome. I've a mountain of food on. Sure why don't you phone over and get Martin to come and bring the babas as well? There's an idea.

MAB. Oh God, you wouldn't want that clatter. (*All swanky.*) We're all going out for our tea tonight.

MA. Mab you told me you were staying.

MAB. Did I?

MA (*hiding her annoyance*). Never worry yourself.

MAB. The New City Hotel if you don't mind. All thirteen of us. The McGintys en masse. They won't know what's hit them.

MA. Very nice.

MAB. So it is. That's where the launch is Ruth. Very posh. Well posh for Derry. We'll get our glad rags on that night girls and show them all a thing or two!

MA. I hear it's very pricey.

MAB (*opening the door*). You should be keeping our books Dolores. Anything to save us from that awful temp. Bee-Bee Moore and her delusions of adequacy. You want to see the state of her Ruth. Sunbeds. Head on her like a scrotum.

RUTH. Mab.

DOPHIE *is making for the open door.*

MA. Mammy SIT!!!

DOPHIE *sidles off into the hot-cupboard.*

You better go quick then Mab, if you're going, before I have a whole handling with this one.

MAB. Sure you'll be sick of the sight of me from now on. (*To* RUTH.) I'll give you a call in the morning – talk shop. See yees girls. (*Exiting.*) Hi Dolores, you'd want to be putting a bit of meat on them two.

Exit MAB.

MA *closes the door behind her and noisily strikes* MAB*'s place-setting.* RUTH *and* AILEEN *sit in silence.* MA *starts carving. She heaps a mountain of meat on to a plate and puts it down in front of* RUTH.

MA. Mammy do you think you could come to the table and we could aim for some semblance of normality?

DOPHIE re-emerges from the hot-cupboard, no longer wearing the nightie, carrying her purse. AILEEN stifles giggles.

What?!

AILEEN. Nothing. Just your mother is standing behind you doing the Dance of the Seven Veils.

DOPHIE. I took it off.

MA. So I see. Well put it back on or you'll have me done for neglect. And then please come to this table and at least *feign* a family meal.

DOPHIE. I've some business to attend to first.

She tips all the change from her purse on to the table.

MA. What are you at now?!

DOPHIE (*sliding one coin, then another, over to* MA). There. That's for you.

MA. You are too kind. Sit.

DOPHIE (*sliding two more coins over to* AILEEN). And that's for the young one.

AILEEN. Cheers. Who's the big pile in the middle for?

DOPHIE (*nodding at* RUTH). That other one of course.

AILEEN. Didn't you do well for yourself? There must be nearly eighty pee there.

MA. I'll have to set up a trust fund. Now that is enough Mammy. All this food is going cold.

She sweeps all the coins off the table into her hand. DOPHIE roars at her.

DOPHIE. Leave that you!

MA halts.

(*Pointing at* RUTH.) She always does well for herself, that one. She knows how. Very cute. I have her now but.

MA. I will not have you ruin this dinner –

DOPHIE. Well I have you now, my girl. You took all of my money and then you went away. To America.

RUTH. Who did? What is she talking about?

MA. She's raving. She's not at herself at all –

DOPHIE. I am completely at myself Dolores. Thank you.

The use of her name takes MA *aback.*

DOPHIE (*to* RUTH). You couldn't have stayed and worked in a factory any more than she could, could you?

RUTH. Who? Catherine?

MA. Could be, or the man on the moon. Mammy –

DOPHIE. You have that same look about you. Flighty. At least she was honest. She always said she was getting out, first chance she got. I just never believed she'd do it. But I believed you, old fool that I am. Daylight robbery. That was every penny I ever had. Every penny.

RUTH. Dophie, I never robbed your money.

DOPHIE. You can't rob what a body *gives* you.

MA. I want a *normal* dinner!

RUTH (*totally confused*). What is –

DOPHIE. Every shiny penny.

MA. Aileen take her up to bed. (*Advancing.*) Upstairs you. This minute.

DOPHIE *cowers in fear of another slap.*

(*Wounded*). Jesus I'm not going to hit you. I'm not going to hit you Mammy.

MA *has to yield and* DOPHIE *continues.*

DOPHIE. You said it was what you wanted. You wanted it to stay. To set up your wee dress-maker's shop and use what we taught you. Make us proud. I taught you to sew. On plastic bags when you were six. Oh you managed to con me all right. My weemin's money.

MA. Mammy leave the wean alone, would you? She's enough on her plate without you – Aileen –

AILEEN *rises.*

RUTH. Hang on, I want to hear this.

DOPHIE. Didn't want your life here at all. As soon as that money had dirtied your paws you were gone. (*Sliding all the coins over to* RUTH.) Well you can take that too. And that's the last of your gettins, and me cleaned out, so you can just leave me in peace now.

MA. Right. If that's the family's millions bequeathed and bequested, maybe you could leave us all in peace now?

DOPHIE. My pleasure. (*Rising to go.*) I wasn't too fussed on the company anyway.

She stops by the nightie on the floor.

And I'm not putting that on my back. Having you think you're doing an old woman a favour with flounces she's hardly fit to wear. I paid for that. *I* did. And dearly. You couldn't count the cost.

Exit DOPHIE *with* AILEEN.

MA *strikes* DOPHIE*'s place setting.*

RUTH. What was that Mammy?

MA. That Ruth, was just a little sampling of the wanton babble this household is ransom to these days. Get used to it.

RUTH. Really. It seemed pretty lucid to me.

MA. Did it now? And what would you know about it? With your big spág just in the door.

RUTH. She was talking about the money you wouldn't let me ask her for so I could stay. Wasn't she? I remember her calling it that. Her weemin's money. Why does she think I got it?

MA. Why does she think *anything* Ruth? She's deranged.

RUTH (*without fully realising the weight of the question*). Did she give you that money for me?

MA. Jesus Christ Ruth! How could you even *ask* that?

RUTH (*aghast*). Sorry. I'm sorry Mammy.

MA. What sort of a monster do you think I am?

RUTH (*genuine*). I said I was sorry.

MA. This is all I need. Two deluded grande-dames in me house now.

Beat – There is silence at the table as RUTH *tries to eat.*

RUTH. This is gorgeous Mammy.

MA. Well eat up. There's *plenty* more.

Beat.

RUTH. She would have let me have it though, if you'd let me ask her.

MA. Jesus Christ Ruth, do you *want* a rise? And you did ask her, if I remember rightly, and just what did that get you? Eh?

RUTH. I got *hinting* at her once. And she was well on for it. Till you told me to shut my beak and never bring the subject up again. In no uncertain terms.

MA *laughs.*

MA. And you could have kept asking her for it Ruth till you were blue in the face and you would *never* have prized a single penny out of her. All you'd have done was upset her. And got your hopes up. I was protecting both of you. And what is more you couldn't *wait* to get going out the door. And who could blame you?

RUTH. What?! You *shovelled* me out it as fast as you could! I wanted –

MA. *Champing* at the bit you were. All we heard out of you for weeks was 'When I'm in America this' and 'when I'm in America that.' And sure it was only natural for you to go. Half your school year was heading over that summer.

RUTH. That doesn't make it natural. I wanted to stay.

MA. There was no stopping you Ruth. Certainly nothing I could have done.

RUTH. Nothing you tried anyway. I like your little jackanory version of events! I did not want to go *at all* and you could have helped me.

MA. With what Ruth? My magic Widow's pension and Child Allowance?

RUTH. With Dophie's money!

MA. That money wasn't mine to give you!

RUTH. It would have taken me *one* year to pay it back. With interest. Instead of going to the States for fifteen. All you had to do was take a very small chance on me. Had you no faith? I had orders in for half the town's First Holy Communion dresses and I hadn't even opened yet! It would have worked. One year. And Dophie would have given it to me if you'd let me ask her!

MA. Honest to God Ruth, I could *string you up!*

Enter AILEEN.

AILEEN. Still playing happy families?

MA. Your dinner's congealing. (AILEEN *is putting on her coat.*)
Where do you think you're going?!

AILEEN. Dunno. Maybe I'll join the McGintys at the City. See
if they'll adopt me.

Exit AILEEN.

RUTH (*trying to throw oil on*). She'll be back in a minute. She's
only away out for a fag.

MA. Do you think I don't know *rightly* where she's going?
(*Scraping* AILEEN's *plate into the bin.*) You're not making
much of a dint in that, are you?

RUTH. It's lovely.

RUTH *chews and 'Mmmns' but can't swallow. She gives in
and puts her fork down.*

RUTH. I'm sorry Mammy, it's just the jet-lag. My stomach
thinks it's time for cornflakes.

MA *snatches the plate off her.*

MA. You and your American notions. Gimme that. (*Scraping the
plate.*) It wasn't pocket money you were looking for Ruth. It
was one hefty sum.

RUTH. Two thousand pounds. Nothing but a really bad week for
me now.

MA. Your attitude to money Ruth is despicable.

RUTH. It would have been the best investment ever. And my life
could have been –

MA (*coming back for the lamb*). Me me me. You haven't
changed a bit. Your life! It looks like a pretty good life from
where I'm sitting.

RUTH. Mammy don't do that!

MA. I'm putting it in the fridge Ruth. You Missy have had all
the opportunity in the world and all that's required of you
now is that you move one step on, not back, on, from where
me and my mother and her mother and so on, had to halt.
That's the natural order of things. Make a fist of it Ruth, the
bloody good cards you were dealt.

RUTH. They're not that bloody good! Ask *Matt!* If you'd helped
me to stay in the first place it could all have been so much
better and different for *all* of us!

MA. That is utter whimsy Ruth! What it *would* have been, is you
struggling day and night trying to get a thruppence ha'penny

business *off the ground* in a depressed town, living heads and thraws in some wee council house somewhere, and a clatter of weans probably, and the likes of Baps McGettigan to thank for them! Would that have been 'better' do you think?

RUTH. Maybe.

MA. Me foot. Here – (*Taking a box of cornflakes out of the press and throwing it down on the table.*) – help yourself. You were always very good at that.

Exit MA to sitting room.

RUTH. Oh Mother Ireland – always so hard put upon! Go away and put your sack-cloth on and give yourself a good flogging! (*Pause.*) And another thing! You were never asked, or expected, to fork out for plane tickets to my wedding! (*No reply.*) Do you hear me? Even if it would have killed you to take it off me! You just love playing the martyr don't you?!

MA (*off-stage*). Hope you enjoy playing the spinster as much.

RUTH (*to herself*). Jesus Christ.

RUTH *knocks the cornflakes box on to the floor. She lifts a glass of flat champagne and toasts herself.*

RUTH. Welcome home Ruthie.

Enter DOPHIE.

She checks and sees that MA is gone, lifts her egg-in-a-cup and sits down at the table to eat it. She gets diverted by the spoon and stops to study herself upside-down in it. RUTH watches quietly. Lights fade.

Blackout.

Interval.

PART TWO

Scene Three

Lights up. It is approximately a week later – the day of the launch. An exquisite cream linen dress hangs in cellophane against the back wall. MA *is ironing a salmon-pink suit.*

Enter RUTH *and* MAB, *a flurry of excitement.* RUTH *is carrying a parcel.*

MAB (*mid-flow*). And a red carpet! Can you believe there's going to be a red carpet?

RUTH. I certainly can Mabs. You ordered it.

MAB. And the paparazzi and the International Press! I'm some operator. Dolores! I wouldn't know you with your face on.

MA. Well I thought I'd honour the occasion. (*To* RUTH.) It's all going well then down below?

RUTH. Like the clappers. You want to see this one in action. In her element, aren't you? Compared to me anyway. I still don't know where anything is even, and spent the whole afternoon just getting in everybody's road. Until I was eventually given a discreet nod from Bee-Bee Moore to make my exit.

MAB. The cheek of her. Oh she thinks she has herself well ensconced, oul vulva-face.

RUTH. Great to know you're so indispensable, isn't it?

MAB. And the cut of Gina Quigley and Jacinta Chambers hemming all afternoon in their curlers and face-packs. No hem on their own skirts mind you, hardly a skirt between them. Those things they'd on would hardly cover a tampon string.

RUTH. Mab would you ever listen to yourself!

MAB. I know. Oul houl' the diddies. I hope they get the night they're looking for. *Pandemonium* Dolores in the staff loos when we were packing up. Them all in fighting to get their slap on in one wee tiny mirror. We'll have to get more mirrors. You couldn't breathe in the place for the hairspray and the Bacardi fumes. And the *slaggin*'!

RUTH. You of course in the thick of it all.

MAB. Aye. (*Feigning annoyance.*) 'Give it up McGinty, sure you'd a face on you like an Ulster fry when you left, and now you're back with extra liver.' The craic was ninety.

RUTH. It all went fairly quiet when I went in.

MAB. Well that's because you're the boss.

RUTH. So are you. And I'm the one who's always nice to them.

MAB. That's the difference between PR in Derry and PR in the States Ruth. 'Nice' doesn't cut it with these girls. Can you dish it, and take it, is all they all want to know, and then everybody knows where they stand.

Beat.

RUTH. I wish I was just one of them – just going out for a night's craic. Are you not nervous Mab?

MAB. What about? Are you? I canny wait.

MA. Sure you must have been through this a hundred times before Ruth. And bigger.

RUTH. I know. I have. But it's a lot scarier on home turf. This is the big one Mammy. This one's not just about sales. Is it?

Beat.

MA (*to* MAB). Could they not all go home and do that?

RUTH. Do what?

MA. Get dressed.

MAB. And end up putting weans' dinners out? (*Lifting her bag to go.*) It's a big do. The only reason I offered to give this one a lift home is so my Martin'll have it all done by the time I get back. Mind you – I'm cutting it a bit short for tarting myself. Am I picking youse up?

MA. Don't be daft. There's too many of us. I've the taxi ordered.

MAB. Fashionably late girls. Fashionably late. I want an entrance.

Exit MAB.

(*Off-stage.*) A red carpet.

RUTH (*laughing*). She told me to expect a standing ovation. She'll have all the McGintys primed and planted and all. You'd think the pair of us were getting married or something. (*A bad reminder – pause.*) Were there any phonecalls for me?

MA. No. Were you expecting any?

RUTH. Not really.

MA. Sorry.

RUTH. Doesn't matter. I just thought he might have called to wish me luck. (*Pause.*) Aileen not back from work yet?

MA. No she's not, the tinker. She's another one cutting it fine.

RUTH (*butterflies*). Oh God! Right. What have I to do? I have to –

MA. The water's on all afternoon for youse. Why don't you take yourself off and get into the bath?

RUTH. Haven't time now. And I need to eat something.

MA. I thought this was a big slap-up dinner affair?

RUTH (*cutting herself some bread and cheese*). It is. I need sustenance now though. Where's Nana?

MA (*smiling*). She's upstairs putting make-up on her. I haven't seen her do that for ten years. Aileen gave her some.

RUTH (*soft*). Is she?

MA. She's much more on the planet this week. Thank God.

RUTH. I know. No Catherine for days.

MA. Good.

RUTH. I miss her.

MA. Well don't be encouraging her Ruth.

RUTH. Why? What's the story there anyway?

MA (*shrugging it off*). Oh.

RUTH. All right. I'll just have to ask Nana then. Won't I?

MA. Don't trawl her through all that Ruth. She's tortured enough.

RUTH. Why what happened? Tell me.

MA. Well from what I was ever able to piece together about it anyway, she died very young. Same age you are now about. Somewhere in Liverpool it was.

RUTH. Oh my God. (*Pause.*) She never even made it to America?

MA. Not even close.

RUTH. What happened to her G.I.?

MA. Well she went off to England with him anyway, that much I know, and then he was sent to the front I suppose. And never came back. I don't know was he killed in action or just did a flit or what, but he never came back for her.

RUTH. Some Cary Grant.

MA. He was hardly that. Left her working out the rest of her days in a Merseyside sweatshop. Not that she had too many of them left. She died in that factory. Her and about twenty other women. I remember it in the news. The May Day Fire.

RUTH. Oh God.

MA. At least it would have been quick. An inch and a half of threads all over everything.

Beat.

(*Lifting* RUTH's *parcel.*) Is that her suit? Give us a jouk.

RUTH *unwraps it.*

RUTH. They did some job, didn't they?

MA. That they did. And all for an oul woman whose dancing days are definitely numbered. (*Pause – Smiling.*) Aileen had her up on the living room floor earlier practising to one of her old records. God love the critter, she couldn't remember a single sequence. And her that could have wiped the floor with any one of them in her day. I think she remembered just enough to remember she couldn't remember it though. She got very cranky over it all. What's the Alzheimer's Two Step?

RUTH. Eh?

MA. What's the Alzheimer's Two Step?

RUTH. Dunno. What?

MA. One! (*Followed by a confused look.*)

RUTH. Mammy!

MA (*laughing*). Aileen told me that. You have to laugh. Anyway, maybe Mabs's Martin or someone will give her a twirl before she turns into a pumpkin altogether. Does your dress need to be pressed before I turn this off?

RUTH. No, it's grand thanks. I saw to it this morning. It's about the only piece of luggage I've managed to unpack yet. (*Referring to the dress hanging up.*) I love making for people I know. It's like making a tape for someone. It's totally Aileen isn't it?

MA. You don't think it still looks too much like a bridesmaid's dress?

RUTH. I wish you had've let me make you a dress.

MA. What's wrong with me good suit? The price of it and it hardly aired.

RUTH. The plan was to have you all there in Maiden City designs. The McGintys all are.

MA (*trying to laugh it off*). You must have used up a year's supply of material to cover some of them big lumps. There's none of them exactly dainty.

RUTH. Wear your camisole for me at least Mammy.

MA. Not with this Ruth. It clashes.

Beat.

(*Hanging up* DOPHIE*'s suit.*) She wasn't a stone's throw off the age I am now when she started to go you know. And look at her now. Madder than three mad people. (*Pause.*) I find it very difficult to watch sometimes. The woman's robbed. I'll tell you this for nothing, if it ever gets to that with me, youse have my full permission to put me out of my misery. A lock of sleeping tablets or something. Horse pills. Anything.

RUTH. How're you fixed for tomorrow?

MA. Mind you, having said that, I'd break me heart if anything happened to Mammy. And then cremate me.

RUTH, *standing behind* MA, *opens the door to the oven with a 'ready when you are' gesture.*

(*Without turning round.*) I see you young one.

RUTH. Do you *still* have eyes in the back of your head?

MA. Yes. And you're not too big for a clatter.

RUTH (*laughing*). Right. I better go and get myself organised. I thought you always wanted to be buried beside Daddy?

MA. Scatter me up over the top of Grianán of Aileach. Your Daddy'll know where to find me. That's where he proposed to me, you know. Well *nearly* where he proposed to me.

RUTH. I know.

MA. Whit Sunday. Nineteen sixty-seven.

RUTH. I know.

MA. He had to stop *before* the top; his heart must have been bad even then. But even then if I'd known I was getting faulty merchandise I'd still have taken him. He picked me bog cotton along the way. One fine man. (*Catching herself on.*) Would you listen to me? One fine eejit. Go away on and get yourself dolled, or you'll never be out the night at all sitting here listening to the likes of this codswallop.

RUTH *smiles and rises.*

MA. He left us too soon.

RUTH. He'd have been proud of me, wouldn't he? (*Beat.*) Following in his footsteps like he said I would. My own business in the town?

Still no reply.

Wouldn't he?

MA. Yes, Ruth, you carried on exactly where he left off. More than you will ever know.

Beat.

He'd have given his life for you.

RUTH *beams at the praise and exits.*

And did, as good as. Oh Colm Sweeney, my heart is seared.

She tries on the jacket of DOPHIE'*s suit, and stops for a moment to admire* RUTH'*s handiwork, and herself in it.*

(*Taking it off.*) MAMMY! And where is that Aileen one?

Bursting into a flurry of activity, she gets her make-up bag and a hair-brush and starts getting herself ready.

DOPHIE *enters in the night-dress. Her hair has been set, she is made-up and wearing ear-rings.*

DOPHIE. Who do I look like? I look like someone. Who is it?

MA (*softly*). You look beautiful Mammy. Just beautiful.

DOPHIE. But who do I look like?

MA. Like yourself. Like you should look. You look like my Mammy.

DOPHIE. I was never beautiful.

MA. Maybe you've grown into yourself.

DOPHIE. That big man could be here.

MA. Who-what?

DOPHIE. Now. Shining his light.

MA (*tenderly*). Try and hang in with us Mammy. Mammy? For this evening. You've been looking forward to this all week. Longer than that. We all have. Wait till you see this.

She hands DOPHIE *her suit.* DOPHIE *takes a good look at it.*

MA. She's a credit to us isn't she? Go up and put it on you. And the blouse and underwear that's laid out on your bed. (*Smiling.*) And your dancing shoes.

RUTH comes running in in her dress.

RUTH (*panicked*). I need a needle and thread, quick! I'm after putting my heel through the hem!

DOPHIE (*taken aback*). Look at her! (*To* MA.) Look!

MA (*smiling*). I see her. I'll get you the sewing box.

DOPHIE. Look. Rita Hayworth. Definitely our side of the house.

RUTH. I still have to put my face on for the full effect.

DOPHIE (*to* MA). She *is* a credit to us, isn't she?

RUTH looks to MA *for a response.* MA *hands her a needle and thread.*

MA. Here.

RUTH (*deflated*). Thanks.

As RUTH *threads the needle,* DOPHIE *watches her intently.*

DOPHIE. Though maybe not our side of the house. Anymore. She'd put you in mind of Colm too, wouldn't she?

RUTH. Daddy?

MA. I always said that.

DOPHIE. Around the eyes. It's in the eyes. I'm only seeing it now.

MA. I see it all the time. It's hard to have them look at me sometimes.

RUTH. Really?

Beat.

Now they both watch RUTH *sew.*

Beat.

(*Self-conscious.*) OK, who are youse looking at? Me or Daddy?

MA. Well it's nice to have him here with us.

RUTH *and* MA *share a smile.*

RUTH. OK.

MA (*softly*). He should be here.

Beat.

I still turn around sometimes and think I see him, sitting there with his cardigan and his hair full of icing sugar.

Beat.

He should be here.

DOPHIE. What are you looking at me for?

MA. What?

DOPHIE. Don't be looking at me Dolores. I'm sick of you shifting it on to me.

MA. I'm not – stay with us Mammy.

RUTH (*finishing the sewing*). There now. Disaster diverted.

DOPHIE (*snapping*). Did you learn nothing at this knee? Did you not? Your pride, Dolores. That's what killed him. Your pride –

MA. What?

RUTH. Dophie –

DOPHIE. and stubbornness! My only child and you wouldn't take a thing off me. Not even to save him. That's how much you hate me, isn't it?

MA. Hate?

RUTH. Please –

MA. Hate? (*Pause.*) When you are so hate-*full*. (*Viciously.*) There are some things I will quite happily let you rewrite in your dotage, anything for a smooth sailing, but *not* that! Do you hear me? *Never* that!

DOPHIE. Have it your own way.

MA*'s back is well up.*

MA. My *own* way? I never got *anything* my own way –

RUTH. Mammy, *now*'s a really good time for a smooth sailing –

MA. Certainly not *that*! There's not *one minute* of that time *I* misremember. Don't you *dare* try and mould it now into something comfortable for you to live with. Not Colm's memory. You don't deserve comfort!

RUTH. Mammy –

DOPHIE. I had the wherewithal. You wouldn't take it!

MA. Ha! Not when the first time it was ever offered me was the day he *died*! 'For a good brass and oak coffin Dolores, there, there.' Never *before* Mammy, *not once* before. Damn all good it was to us then. You had to let it go that far didn't you? And then offering your thirty pieces of silver to ease your guilt. I'd rather him buried in cardboard.

DOPHIE. I offered it plenty!

MA. Yes. Yes you did. You tried to pass it off again the day we put him into the ground. 'For a holiday Dolores, you need one!' And again a week later. And again at his Month's Mind. 'Take it off me Dolores, please!' – *Absolve* me Dolores – 'Put it back into the business then!' Or 'Give it to the wean for her shop, or to the – '

RUTH. What?

DOPHIE. I didn't want you to lose them both.

RUTH. What?

MA. – but *never* when it counted. Never. I should have thrown it into the ground with him. That's what I should have done with that bloody money!

RUTH. What did you do with it?

MA. *Facts* Mammy. Not your version, not my version, just the facts – no matter how much they rankle you. So are we clear now, or do you want it spelled out some more?

DOPHIE *can't reply.*

Enter AILEEN, *oblivious.*

AILEEN. I know! I know! Don't anybody say anything to me! Not after the day I've had. I'll be ready in two ticks, I swear!

She grabs her dress and runs up the stairs.

MA (*shovelling the suit at* DOPHIE). Get upstairs and get dressed. Go! Get out of my sight.

DOPHIE *exits.*

RUTH. *I'd* like it spelled out some more.

MA (*putting a full stop on it*). A smooth sailing Ruth. A smooth sailing.

RUTH. Except that the wind is up.

MA. Then pipe down. This is for you.

RUTH *laughs.*

RUTH. I'm glad something is.

MA (*sewing box*). Are you finished?

RUTH. Not quite. She did give you that money for me, didn't she?

MA. Well unless you're deaf Ruth, I'd have thought that was fairly obvious by now.

RUTH. Why didn't you give it to me?

MA *ignores her.*

Mammy!

MA. In the circumstances Ruth, I just couldn't help myself.

RUTH. Well quite obviously you did!

MA. Did I indeed? My God.

She gets up and roots out an old bank-book from the depths of the sideboard.

(*Throwing it down on the table.*) There you are. Every bloody penny! All intact. Take it. I couldn't touch it. It's like a disease.

RUTH. Again, too bloody late to do any good. Isn't it? Why did you lie to me? Why didn't you let me have it?

MA. I told you Ruth, in my fibre I just couldn't.

RUTH. Jesus you knew how I wanted to –

MA. For God's sake Ruth! Can we not just bury the hatchet on something that happened lifetimes ago and just move on? Do you have to make a mountain of everything?

RUTH. This *is* a mountain! You kept that from me and you lied. Did you not want me here? Did you not?

No reply.

RUTH. You didn't mind losing both of us at all did you?

MA. Ruth –

RUTH. I don't think you even want me back *now*. And it didn't happen lifetimes ago. It's all *still* happening. That's the bloody problem! Look at the state of me and you. And you constantly turning it all back on me, that I made this mess all by myself, that I couldn't even 'make a decent fist of the

cards fate dealt me.' *You* dealt them! You hypocritical oul –
you turned my whole life inside out for the sake of just two
thousand pounds! And then tried to blame *me!* I was just a
wean for God's sake – *yours!*

MA. I can understand Ruth, why Mammy wouldn't part with it.
I don't like her for it, but I understand. I couldn't house her
otherwise. Maybe now you need to extend some of that to
me.

RUTH. I would. Gladly. But maybe you need to give me a good
reason first. Two thousand pounds worth.

MA. You don't understand worth at all, do you? Or cost.
Dophie's right about that. It wasn't just *any* two thousand
pounds Ruth. I grew up with that money, and I knew its
worth all my life. Our 'perpetual succour', Mammy called
it. No matter what befell us 'We'll be all right, haven't we
money in the bank' was her constant creed. It never came out
of the bank, mind you. Maybe if it had it would have been
just two thousand pounds in no time. Just money. And
Mammy thought she'd never be able to pull us through
another bad patch if it was gone, spent on getting us through
the last one. So she never touched it.

DOPHIE *comes down and sits on the bottom stair, unnoticed
by* MA *and* RUTH. *All the audience sees is her stockinged legs.*

Not when her *own* husband died, or when she was laid off, or
when I was, and not for Colm either. I *begged* her for that
money Ruth, to bail him out. I sat in that very chair (*Da's
chair.*) and cried and pleaded and prayed at her for weeks on
end to help us. But she wouldn't budge. Too scared. Kept her
fist wrapped around it as tight as ever she did. Bloody money,
impotent from the very beginning. That was Catherine's life
savings – she tried to use it once to come home again, but
Dophie wouldn't let her back in. Another one that woman
sent to an early grave.

DOPHIE *slides her hands over her knees, holds her ankles
and begins to rock.*

She just kept telling me he could pull himself out, hadn't he
done it before, wouldn't he do it again, there there, don't fret
yourself pet – right up until the priest came to the door to tell
me he was dead. 'But we'll be all right Dolores, haven't we
money in the bank?' He *worried* himself to *death*, Ruth, for
the want of *just* two thousand pounds. Worried about his
workers, that he'd be leaving them and their families in
trouble. Insisted on going in to work, and him under doctor's

orders to stay in bed. There's still women in this town who wouldn't pass me without a nod and I don't know them Ruth, but they worked for your father and know I was married to one of the most decent men this town ever saw. Even half that money might have saved him. But she just had to hang on to it. A few measly bob. 'That's weemin's money Dolores. That's weemin's money.' And what was I only her daughter?

RUTH. And what am I only yours?

MA. I *nearly* had it off her Ruth. *Nearly* had it in my hand while there was still time, until you waded in that is, all wide-eyed and innocent, and had to ask for it. The apple of her eye. Not that you would have got it off her either, but you gave her an out and by God she took it. A welcome stall for her. And a fortnight later she was still stalling and your father dead.

RUTH. We didn't even know that Daddy was sick or in trouble! You protected us from all that!

MA. Maybe if you hadn't been standing there with your hand out you might have *seen* what was going on.

RUTH. You can't blame me!

MA. No. (*Pause.*) But I couldn't let you have the money either.

Beat.

RUTH (*slowly*). I can understand that. What you did in grief. And I'd love to see us move on Mammy. All this is awful. I just need to hear you say that you didn't do it to me on purpose. That's all. (*Pause.*) Mammy?

Beat.

It would make it a lot easier for you to house me. If you want me here.

Pause.

Do you want me here?

No reply.

(*Hissing.*) Your mother's daughter. You're as bad as each other.

DOPHIE *can't take it anymore. She enters wearing only the blouse and her tights.*

DOPHIE (*a plaintiff low*). Ohhhhhhh –

She blasts the taps.

RUTH. Can you not see that?

MA (*jumping up*). Mammy? Oh no.

DOPHIE. Ohhhhhhh –

RUTH. You can, can't you? And you don't like it one bit. She wouldn't give it to you, so you wouldn't give it to me.

DOPHIE. Ohhhhhhhhhhhh –

MA (*to* RUTH). Now look what you've done.

RUTH. *I've* done? You're so skilled at apportioning blame.

MA *turns the taps off and tries to hold* DOPHIE.

MA. How long has she been standing there? (*Rocking* DOPHIE, *but she won't accept the comfort.*) Shssh. There, there. It's over Mammy. It's all over now.

RUTH (*turning the taps back on*). Ha!

MA. Ruth! Turn those off! Do you not think there's enough damage done already?

But MA *feels the change in* DOPHIE*'s body and has to yield to* RUTH*'s judgement. Once* DOPHIE *is quietened,* MA *flicks off the taps again.*

She'll have them taps bled dry.

RUTH (*going to* DOPHIE). I think it's herself she's trying to bleed.

MA. Leave her. I'll take her.

MA *takes her and brings her to a chair.* DOPHIE *is compliant, a blank expression on her face. She has completely absented herself.*

I'm sorry Mammy.

RUTH. Tell me Mammy. (*Pause.*) Two words.

She can't.

AILEEN *bounds down the stairs.*

AILEEN. De-nah! (*Doing a twirl.*) I'm a swan! I'm a swan! Am I a ride or what? Are youse not dressed yet? What's keeping youse? It's nearly half. Come on! We'll show 'em what the Sweeneys are made of, will we not girls?! Nana, tell me you're not going out in your drawers please? Maybe we should leave the underwear modelling to the under sixty-fives, eh?

MA. Aileen.

AILEEN. Or do you think could you still pass the pencil test Nana?

MA. Aileen.

AILEEN. Sure I could nearly park one of my vans in under there.

MA. Aileen.

AILEEN. What?

Nobody speaks. The taxi horn blares outside.

What's wrong? (*Seeing* DOPHIE *properly for the first time.*) What is it? What's wrong with Nana?

MA. Just all the excitement of tonight got too much for her is all. Don't fret yourself. She's just worn out.

AILEEN. Oh no.

MA. She'll be grand in the morning.

AILEEN. After all our dance practice.

MA. Come on Mammy, I'll take you up.

AILEEN. What? Are you not going either?

MA. I can't leave her with strangers. Not like this.

AILEEN. But you can't not go Mammy. You have to be there. Doesn't she Ruth?

RUTH. It would have been nice.

MA. You two go on and enjoy yourselves.

AILEEN. Oh no. This is terrible. Nana?

MA. Leave her pet please.

Taxi horn again.

Youse better go on. Go.

AILEEN. Och Mammy –

MA. You don't want to be late do you?

AILEEN. But –

MA. Aileen, maybe I'll get a taxi down in a wee while, after I get her over, how's that? Now go on will you? You look lovely.

AILEEN (*kissing her gingerly*). All right then. Bye Nana. (*To* RUTH *from the door.*) You right? (*To* MA.) We'll keep you a seat.

Exit AILEEN.

MA. So do you.

RUTH. What?

MA. Look lovely.

RUTH *lifts the scissors and undoes the stitches in her hem. Then she goes to* DOPHIE *and kisses the top of her head. She goes to the door stopping by* MA *on her way.*

RUTH. You're not going to come are you?

No answer.

I'm sorry you won't be there. I've lived this night out in my head a million times and you've been there in every version. Proud of me. That picture's half of what got me here you know.

Another impatient blast from the taxi.

MA. You better go.

RUTH *waits, hoping for something more. Nothing. She lifts* MA*'s lipstick, puts some on and about to leave, stops again.*

RUTH. Can you not even tell me you're proud of me?

Nothing.

Exit RUTH, *slamming the door behind her.*

Beat.

MA*'s eyes come to rest on* DOPHIE.

MA. Oh Mammy.

She sits at the table beside her and strokes her hair.

What are you thinking about? What goes on inside that head of yours at all, eh?

Beat.

I used to while away *hours* wondering that exact same thing about Ruth and Aileen when they were babies.

Beat.

If there's one thing I did right in this world it was produce the two of them. Eh?

Beat.

I made a big mistake, didn't I? A big mistake.

Beat.

Come back. I need me Mammy.

Slow fade to blackout.

Scene Four

Low lights up. It is the middle of the same night. DOPHIE is alone on stage, sitting half-way up the stairs in her dressing-gown.

Enter RUTH, switching on the light. Her hackles are clearly up. She takes off her coat, clears the table and throws the scissors into the sewing box. She stops in her tracks at the sink and lifts out a bouquet of flowers. She reads the card.

RUTH. Yellow orchids. (*She smells them – then upset.*) Bastard. Did it have to be the yellow orchids?

She crams the whole lot in the bin. She pulls out her portfolio and rifles through it. DOPHIE watches her, not sure about coming down into this. RUTH catches sight of her.

Dophie. Are you all right?

DOPHIE. I was waiting for you.

RUTH. No sleepies? (DOPHIE *shakes her head.*) Are you coming down?

DOPHIE (*sitting tight*). Were you dancing?

RUTH. I danced.

DOPHIE *starts to hum one of her Tommy Dorsey tunes, and comes down the stairs. She dances for a few bars in the kitchen.*

DOPHIE. I married a beautiful dancer you know. We just *swooned* out on to the floor. Not like some of the ones has to be always counting into your ear. Beautiful dancer. But an awful dour man. My daughter married a fine man. You'll like him. Twinkly eyes. He's not here at the minute. He does his deliveries at this time you see. He's a baker. (*Puffed up.*) He supplies to nearly everyone in the town you know. Did you have any children?

RUTH. No.

DOPHIE. That must be sore for you. You who always wanted your quickenings. But you're still in your blossom-time yet. And you'd make a lovely mother, sure weren't you mine?

RUTH. I'm not so sure I do want it anymore. You need skills. I'd be afraid now of keeping things in perpetuity.

DOPHIE. You've nothing to be scared of. Just don't let her harden you or it *will* all keep going round and round. All this for just an accident. Don't let her keep you in his shadow any more.

RUTH. Baby Francis?

DOPHIE. Mammy shouldn't have left an infant still in its swaddling sleeping on a big bed like that. Where anything could happen to it.

RUTH. I suppose it was easier for her to blame me.

DOPHIE. Yes. (*Pause.*) She said it was because you forgot to slip the stitches in his christening gown. Yes. She had plenty of ways to make you feel the blame.

RUTH. She must have been in a lot of grief.

DOPHIE. Yes. She never cried.

Beat.

Have you a photograph?

RUTH. A photograph?

DOPHIE. Of your husband?

RUTH. Oh. Am –

Unsure, RUTH *takes a photo of Matt out of her bag and hands it to* DOPHIE.

DOPHIE. What's his name?

RUTH. Matt.

DOPHIE. Mathew. Good solid name. Isn't he handsome? I love a broad shoulder. Twinkly eyes too. And look Catherine! Niagara Falls! Well, didn't you turn out to be the glamorous pair? Film stars! England would never have done you at all. Is this your honeymoon?

RUTH. Am. . . yes.

DOPHIE. I never got a honeymoon. Niagara Falls. This is a balm to me. Have you one of him in his uniform? I bet he looks even more like Cary Grant in his uniform.

RUTH (*laughing*). No. This is the only one.

DOPHIE. Put it away again safe then. What ilk of a man is he? What's he like?

RUTH. Well, he's more like Jimmy Stewart really.

DOPHIE. We can live with that.

RUTH. And . . . I like a broad shoulder too. Something to get in under. And am – I dunno. He smells right.

DOPHIE. Very important.

RUTH. He smells like my comfort blanket I used to have. Remember?

DOPHIE *smiles and nods.*

DOPHIE. He'll be worried about you now. Don't leave it too long Catherine. Does he dance?

RUTH (*laughing*). Badly. Not that it ever stops him. Nothing stops him.

DOPHIE. Well he could learn.

RUTH (*smiling*). Yes.

DOPHIE. And he makes you smile.

RUTH *can only nod.*

DOPHIE (*smiling*). That's everything then. (*Getting up to go.*) I'll rest now.

RUTH. Dophie?

DOPHIE. I'll sleep now. (*Stopping.*) One time I was paddling in the Atlantic you know. On a day trip we took to Malin Head. When I was little and you were gone. And I thought to myself 'Imagine, Catherine could be paddling in this here Atlantic too!' And it would be like we were just in a big bath together. As close as that.

RUTH *watches her go up the stairs.*

See? As close as that. It doesn't have to be that far lamb. In your heart. It doesn't have to.

She's gone.

RUTH *sits still a moment lost in thought, surveys the room, then gets up and flicks off the light.*

Blackout.

Scene Five

In the black we hear footsteps approaching the back door. There is a sound of giggling and a key turning in the lock. Someone stumbles in. MAB's *and* AILEEN's *voices in Yankee drawls are heard over their mobile phones.*

MAB (*outside*). Chris to Kelly! COME IN KELLY! I can't see where the fuck I'm going! Get a bloody light on! Do you read?

AILEEN. Loud and clear Chris. I'm on the case. Keep your Big Hair on! Over and out.

There is the sound of a crash.

MAB. Are you on your arse again?

AILEEN. Yip.

MAB. Ah well, you must be getting used to it by now. (*Fumbling around.*) I can't find you.

RUTH *flicks on the light.* AILEEN *has knocked over the bread bin, contents everywhere, and is lying drunk beside it.* MAB *is on all fours looking for her.*

RUTH. Well well well.

MAB (*jumping*). Jesus fuckin' diddies Ruth, you scared the hole out of me!

RUTH. That's just lovely that is.

MAB. Oh we're so genteel.

RUTH. Not that. Demoting me to Sabrina in my absence. Didn't take youse long to forget about me.

MAB. Well you were the one insisted on leaving early.

AILEEN. And you still turned into a pumpkin! (*She kills herself laughing at this.*) Kelly to Chris. I have just made a very important discovery. Jammy Dodgers, a soda and half a pan –

MAB (*lifting slices off the floor*). Mother's Pride! You couldn't bate the stuff! Bags the heel! Get the kettle on there.

AILEEN *goes about trying to co-ordinate tea and toast for everyone.*

RUTH. Had a little drink then Mabs?

MAB. Course I didn't. This is just my natural exuberance. Come on – toast! FEED ME! Excuse me – feed *us*. It's great isn't it? Nine months of purely medicinal pigging out on doctor's orders.

AILEEN. So much for the Angelus then, eh?

MAB. I know. The Lord moves in mysterious ways. Madonna and Child or what?! It's been some night all round hasn't it?

RUTH. Hasn't it just.

AILEEN. You never gave us the whole story Mab, what Martin said to you.

MAB. Och he's as lured so he is. (*Pause.*) Even if he doesn't know it yet. He'll be grand. (*Laughing.*) A bit of coaxing is all he needs.

RUTH. Since a bit of conning is all it took.

MAB. Sometimes a girl just has to take what she wants in this world.

RUTH. I suppose she does.

MAB. And I don't have too many breeding years left in me.

RUTH. You're the same age as me!

MAB. Exactly. (*To* AILEEN.) What's keeping you Sweeney? I'm going to fade away.

RUTH. As if. I'd kill for a bagel right now. A pumpernickel bagel and cream cheese.

AILEEN. With Mother's Pride in the house?!

MAB. And Dairylea?!

RUTH. Yum yum.

AILEEN. Nyah nyah. *Pumpernickel bagels.* All we've had out of you all week is pumpernickel bagels.

RUTH. Eh?

AILEEN. Aye. And 'the Irish just think if they slap coleslaw all over something then it's good food' and 'it's never this hard to get a taxi in the States' and 'in the States this would be *half* the price and – '

RUTH. I have not.

AILEEN. You have so.

RUTH. Have I?

MAB. A bit.

AILEEN. And looking for a marghuerita in Roaring Meg's! Sure Babycham's as glamorous as they ever got! Ha! Your idea of home is about as on the money as Dophie's notions of America. Does that not scare you? Because it should you know.

MAB. What happened you anyway?

RUTH. Dunno. Guess the States still has more of a hold on me than I thought. Teething problems.

MAB. Tonight I mean, you eejit. What took you off so early?

AILEEN. I bet the Ma was *fuming* she had to miss it. She'd have been in her element. Swanning around the place like the Mother of the Bride. Oh! Jesus Ruth sorry. I didn't mean to say that.

RUTH. It's quite all right Aileen.

AILEEN. It just slipped out.

RUTH. Aileen, it's all right.

AILEEN. Right. (*Pause.*) But I'm really sorry.

RUTH. Thank you can we have the end of it now please?

MAB. She'd've had some job trying to out-do mine but. (*Posh.*) 'Well my Mabs always had great vision. And *great* assiduity' I don't even know what that means. Neither does she I'm sure. I'm sure the Mayor was riveted. I'm surprised she didn't have my feis medals with her to show around.

AILEEN. What did you win at the feis?

MAB. Nothing. But you know what I mean. 'Vision.' Sure all I ever saw was a dollar sign and me ticket back home. You had all the vision.

RUTH. But you had the neck Mab.

MAB (*chuffed*). What have you there? (*The portfolio.*)

RUTH. Just the finishing touches on the Frankfurt collection.

MAB. *Tonight?* Girlfriend, you've gone on about this night for *years* – could you not just rest still and let yourself enjoy it? You should have stayed for the speeches Ruth. One *tripping* over the other to say something even *more* wonderful about us.

RUTH. Oh I heard them all right. I heard a crowd of women in the loos, ones I went to school with, call me a 'jumped up wee snot.'

MAB (*laughing*). Aye. That's home for you all right.

RUTH. Same bitch has a job application sitting on my desk and all. 'Whatever she thinks of herself coming here and doing this, she's not doing anything we couldn't have done ourselves.' Who's 'we'? I thought I was we.

MAB. Ruth, we sold every single line tonight. To buyers from everywhere. It was a *huge* success.

RUTH. It didn't need to be just a financial success Mabs.

MAB. What? You have to have the love of the common people as well? Don't sicken me happiness Ruth. What are you worried about that for?

RUTH. It's just – it's just that *none* of this is how I imagined it was going to be.

MAB. Oh for God's sake Ruth! This is *it!* You banged on for years about this, about building up a huge business for yourself and bringing yourself back home with it. And that's exactly what we've done. We've *arrived!* Most of the time I just thought you were off your rocker – poor wee Maiden City nothing more than a shared Sunday morning market stall with schizo Sam and his Way-Big Weiners, selling home-made knickers at five bucks a throw and the two of us spending the rest of the week in the Paradise Home up to our oxters in geriatric shite. But you pulled it off Ruth. You pulled it off.

RUTH. *We* pulled it off.

MAB. Well then?

AILEEN. Aye?

MAB. All this because you overheard a bit of gossip in a loo? You think they're not all talking about me too Ruth? 'Jesus didn't that Mab McGinty one do well for herself? And her as thick as pig shit. Who'd a thought she had it in her, eh? All the McGintys was thick as pig shit. They must be as lured.'

AILEEN (*concurring*). Aye!

MAB (*piqued*). I hear them. I wasn't exactly part of the Brain Drain out of here. I'm well aware of that. But here we are Ruth, top of the pile, and they can all go kiss my big hairy hole.

RUTH. Jesus. That's the first demon I ever saw in your closet in my whole life.

MAB (*laughing*). Aye, but he's a lonely wee critter.

RUTH. I'm saying maybe I made a mistake.

Beat.

MAB. Oh.

RUTH. Not in bringing Maiden City home Mabs. That's great. Just maybe in bringing myself back too.

There is silence for a moment. Then AILEEN *turns and heaves into the sink, vomiting copiously.*

MAB. Here I'll hold your hair.

AILEEN. Sorry. (*Wiping her face.*) I guess I'm just sick of listening to you. (*Laughing at her pun*).

RUTH. What the fuck's got into you all night?

She vomits again. When she turns around it is all down the front of the dress.

RUTH. You christened it well anyway. Thanks.

MAB. Champagne, red wine, Carlsberg, Bacardi –

The litany turns AILEEN*'s stomach. They are all on alert. The nausea passes.*

AILEEN. I feel putrid so I do.

RUTH. And you look just beautiful.

MAB. What did you go and drink so much for anyway? You were *lashing* it into you girl.

AILEEN. Obliteration my only aim.

RUTH. What?

AILEEN. I wanted to get out of my head.

RUTH. Well congratulations Aileen.

AILEEN. Well don't mention it Ruth.

MAB *pours her a pint glass of water.*

MAB. Here you, take this, and this (*She gives her a bucket from under the sink.*) and take yourself off to your bed. You're a light-weight, Sweeney.

AILEEN *attempts a retaliation but hasn't the energy.* MAB *and* RUTH *watch her sidle off. Exit* AILEEN.

Weans.

RUTH *sits down.* MAB *joins her.*

This is about Matt isn't it?

No reply.

Did you get your flowers?

RUTH. What?

MAB. He's been on the phone to me every day since you got back. Checking that you're all right. Will you not at least talk to him Ruth?

RUTH *doesn't reply.*

This is very hard for me to get. Even if I am a bit thick. You two are mad about each other, fucksake. I don't know how you thought you could up and leave him *without* feeling like this. (*Pause.*) Maybe you did make a mistake.

RUTH. The mistake I made is a lot bigger than just me and Matt.

MAB. I mean apart from where to live Ruth, and that's just practical, youse never looked to me like youse were having *any* problems. . .

Beat.

RUTH. *I* was. Big ones.

MAB. Really? (*Scandalised.*) What?

Beat.

MAB. What? I never saw any sign of problems.

RUTH. No, well, you wouldn't you see. (*Slowly.*) Every piece of underwear we ever sold Mabs, he had to get prancing around in it first. Probably even the very knickers you've on you now. And a particular penchant for our Summer thong collection. I just couldn't hack it any more.

MAB *is uncharacteristically dumbstruck.* RUTH *laughs.*

MAB. You bitch!

RUTH. For God's sake Mab, it's Matt we're talking about.

The laughing subsides.

MAB. I think he's waiting for you.

RUTH. I doubt it. I did far too much damage.

MAB. I doubt beyond repair.

RUTH. You think not? Do you know what I did Mabs? We were ordering our flowers for the wedding, yellow orchids, and I just walked out of the shop in a blind panic and into the travel agents next door and bought a one-way ticket home. And came back in and put it down on the counter in front of him. Beside the flowers. Just like that. I didn't even say anything. I couldn't. I just left. Made my final decision with a machete. Not much going back after that. Is there?

MAB. Would you?

RUTH. Would you take a cunt like me back?

MAB. Beside the point. I still think he's waiting it out.

RUTH. Did he say that? . . . Did he?

MAB. No. But –

RUTH. No buts. He really doesn't need me Mab. And the Ma needs me *here* like a hole in the head. And Maiden City doesn't *really* need me, and Maiden City Philadelphia *certainly* doesn't need me. What the fuck have I done? I'm a piece of Atlantic flotsam.

MAB's mobile rings. She looks at the screen and mouths 'Martin.'

MAB. Hallo Love of my Life. . . no, I haven't run off with a sailor. . . yes, I'm aware that it's the scrake of dawn. . . no I haven't forgotten that we have a house full of screaming weans. . . yes, I'm on my way, I'm just passing the ah – Bingo Hall now so I am. Two ticks, Sweetness and Light.

She hangs up.

Ooops.

RUTH. You have ballast.

MAB. Don't I just. (*Patting her tummy.*) And more coming. I better make tracks Ruth or I'll be kilt.

RUTH. Of course.

MAB. Come in to me tomorrow.

RUTH (*helping her collect her things*). I just shoulda fallen for a Donegal fella like you. Would have made things a whole lot simpler.

MAB (*laughing*). Oh yeah, much simpler. Go easy on yourself Ruth. It's the wee small hours and you've had a couple. It's not as bad as it seems. Hard yes, but it'll get easier.

RUTH. Thanks.

MAB. You'll see. (*Patting her tummy again.*) Come on little Erin. Time to get you home.

RUTH. You're not really going to call her that are you?

MAB. Certainly am. She might have been conceived over there but she'll be the first of my brood to be born over here. (*With a twinkle.*) And only the first mind you.

RUTH. How do you know it's a she?

MAB. I know.

She smiles, kisses RUTH and exits.

Scene Six

RUTH *closes the door. Dawn is well up by now. She empties the tea-pot into the bin before she remembers about the flowers. She manages to save one unspoilt one.*

She turns off the main light and the stairwell light and heads up. There is a kerfuffle as she passes someone on the stairs.

RUTH. Aileen?

AILEEN. Uhhh.

> AILEEN *puts the light on above the cooker. Blue light. She is banging around the kitchen looking for something.* RUTH *comes back down.*

> Solpadeine.

RUTH *hands her the medicine box.* AILEEN *opens it.*

> Brilliant. Cotton-wool, bonjela and bon-bons. You wouldn't need a medical emergency.

RUTH. Looks like we have one.

> AILEEN *lights up.*

> Is that wise?

AILEEN. Wind your neck down would you? Sure Mabs has been smoking in here all night.

RUTH. Except that she hasn't.

AILEEN. Oh yeah.

She smokes anyway.

RUTH. What if the Ma comes down?

AILEEN. Then she'll see me smoking. Won't she?

RUTH. All we need.

AILEEN. My battle Ruth – it's actually got nothing to do with you – it doesn't *all* have to centre around you, you know.

RUTH. The head on you.

AILEEN. Give us a fucking break, I've to be in work in less than two hours.

> RUTH *gets* AILEEN *some tablets from her handbag and a glass of water.*

RUTH. Here. Codeine something or other. (*Exiting.*) Maybe you should just call it quits and take the day off.

AILEEN. Wouldn't that be nice? Except that the quits were already called *for* me Ruth.

RUTH (*coming back down*). What?

AILEEN. Because, Ruthie, Mr Wilman, our kindly and benevolent neighbourhood bank manager, yesterday announced that he's repossessing our last two vans. (*Raising her cigarette.*) Sound one, Mr Wilman.

RUTH. What? Why didn't you say?

AILEEN. Didn't want to piss on your parade, did I?

RUTH. Oh Aileen –

AILEEN. And he's pulled our mortgage approval –

RUTH. Oh no –

AILEEN. Oh yes. And swiftly followed by the mother of all screaming matches between me and Neil who, I don't know if you even noticed, royally stood me up last night. Fucker.

RUTH. I'm really sorry –

AILEEN. Not that you would. Notice. Too busy idealising my wee business and my wee house and my wee husband – my wee life. Ha! You'd be better off living your own life Ruth. Go ahead. Feel free. Nobody's stopping you, you know. Anything instead of this languishing around here and torturing us all to death with 'I dunno. Will I do *this* or will I do *that* or will I go *here* or will I go *there*?' Lovely to have all the options. Just shit or get off the pot would you Ruth. It's not that complicated. Oh for a pot to shit in – I'm not even going to get out of this house at this rate. For someone who works in transport, I'm certainly feeling very fucking stationary. I'd love to get *married* Ruth. Do you know that? I would *love* to get married. But of course you don't know that – because I'm hardly going to go laying that one on you, not in the circumstances, but you didn't leave me much room to either. Did you? Not that it matters anyway. Neil can't really 'see the point.' 'Not really into that tux and tails shite.' Wants to get the business sorted first, and then the house, and then, and then there'll be something else – wait till you see. But I want it. Nothing swanky. Just your good old white-wedding-turkey-and-ham-dinner. But I've two fuckin' chances now. And then to top it all off that *bag* Bee-Bee Moore comes greasin' up to me in the middle of your speech the night, to 'commiserate with me on the unhappy demise of Fleetfoot Fetch and Carry.' How the fuck did she know?

That *you* didn't doesn't surprise me at all but how the fuck did she know? You can't fart in this town. And 'what a pity Maiden City are being so slow to tender out their transport bids, isn't it? Would you not have had a wee word in the big sister's ear? Too late for you now though, isn't it?'

RUTH. I'll sort that out first thing in the morning.

AILEEN. Will you now? I think it's gone a bit past that stage Ruth, don't you*?* Sort yourself out. I don't need your hand-me-downs and hand-outs forever. Yellow flares is one thing. (*She stubs out her cigarette.*) It wouldn't have saved my bacon anyhow. (*Standing and putting out her hand for more pain-killers.*) Give us some of those yokes for later on.

RUTH (*handing them over*). I'm really sorry Aileen.

AILEEN. Save it. I'm away to get dressed for work. What's left of it.

She exits. RUTH *sits.*

RUTH. And I'll just sit here and stew in my own juices.

She pops a few of the pills herself.

Blackout.

Scene Seven

Next day. A bright sunny afternoon. The stage is empty. There are bold hand-made signs around the set – HOT-CUPBOARD – FRIDGE – STAIRS – BACK DOOR – etc. Orientation signs for DOPHIE.

Two suitcases sit in the middle of the floor.

DOPHIE *enters. She checks on the cases briefly. She takes her stash of bon-bons out of the medicine box and secretes them in her handbag. She sits down at the table and waits, watching out the window. Her head follows the path of a car going up the road. And of another going down. She gets up and tries to open the back door but can't. She goes into the hot-cupboard for her coat.*

Enter RUTH. RUTH *is taking off her coat as* DOPHIE *is putting hers on.*

DOPHIE *re-enters the body of the room. She moves with the excitement and trepidation of a young girl.*

DOPHIE. We'll have to be very careful. We'll have to zig-zag.

RUTH. Zig-zag?

DOPHIE. Submarines.

RUTH. Oh. Of course.

She puts on a hat.

DOPHIE. All the way across the Atlantic. We'll watch the water widen from the dock together this time! Oh America! Cigars and gasoline and Dophie! Oh Catherine my light. I'm on my way over now.

RUTH. Dophie?

DOPHIE. I can't wait. Niagara Falls! Look I'm all ready.

RUTH. So I see. Dophie –

DOPHIE (*sings – Tommy Dorsey's 'I'll be Seeing You'*).
I'll be seeing you
In all the old familiar places
That this heart of mine embraces
All day through –

RUTH. Dophie –

DOPHIE. What?

Beat.

RUTH. Nothing. (*Pause.*) Mickey Rooney's in for a fright.

DOPHIE (*giggling*). Oh no! Don't!

RUTH. If the cigars and the gasoline haven't killed him yet.

DOPHIE. I hope so.

They laugh.

RUTH. Dophie –

DOPHIE. Catherine.

RUTH. Yes. Dophie –

DOPHIE. It's Josephine.

RUTH. What?

DOPHIE. I want you to promise me that when we get there, you'll call me by my proper name. I want it back when we get there. You have to know who you are and where you are, don't you?

RUTH. Yes. (*Pause.*) Yes you do.

DOPHIE. I always call you by your proper name, don't I?

RUTH (*pause*). Yes.

DOPHIE. I come from a line of six Josephines at least but we all got called something else. It's a wonder any of us know who we are at all, isn't it? Or where we come from. And this way we can bring them all with us. Little Women – open the door!

RUTH *guides her gently away from it.*

(*Cross.*) It wouldn't have done for you. Oh no. 'My name isn't Kitty. My name is Catherine.' You were as stubborn, just like your name-sake. (*Pause.*) Poor scorched Saint Catherine. I used to get such awful nightmares, remember, thinking you were going to end up like her, but you'd bring me into your bed and tell me not to be such a silly-face. You were going to America. And live like in the films. A life in Technicolor. And bring me too. (*Beat.*) But I could see it all in my head. It seemed to me like you were only bound to meet the same end. (DOPHIE*'s energy has become jerky, she tries to calm herself.*) But I won't desert you this time I promise. Not this time. (*As she fights with it.*) Open the door.

RUTH. Dophie I can't –

DOPHIE. Oh no – please! Open it!

There is a fierce struggle at the door.

RUTH. Dophie, I can't let you out.

DOPHIE. Please, quick! I won't let it be like the last time!

RUTH (*gently*). Remember what you said? You can go home, but you can't go back?

DOPHIE. Oh no! Let me make my peace! Oh no!

RUTH. Shush Dophie.

DOPHIE. Poor Saint Catherine. In the wrong place at the wrong time so they set fire to her. Tied her to a wheel and sent her spinning round through the flames. Spinning round and round. I saw it all in my head. Catherine on a wheel. Going round. And round. And round. I saw it all.

RUTH. Dophie –

DOPHIE (*starting to spin*). Lots of little stars shooting off her! Weeee! Up into the night sky – all the way up to the stars! Weeeeee! Hollywood starlets!

MA *enters from the living room.*

MA. Mammy? Ruth! What have you –

DOPHIE. All the way up! Weeeeeee! (*Becoming hysterical.*) Straight up and no kiss! No night-night kiss for Dophie!

MA. Mammy –

DOPHIE. Up to Baby Francis now! Back where it all started.

MA. I *told* you not to be grilling her Ruth!

DOPHIE. Kisses for Francis but Dophie doesn't deserve a kiss. Oh God! I'm so sorry Catherine! All the threads stuck to your hair! Sucking up the flames! Whoosh! Don't go! Somebody open a door! Somebody! (MA *thinks to calm her by turning on the taps – this only aggravates her more.*) Water couldn't quench this! Calico and cotton – whoosh! – yards and yards and bales and bales of it – whoosh! A funeral pyre. All my fault. I sent you to it. I'm sorry Catherine. I'm so sorry. Your beautiful hair. The smell of it. (*The air finally going out of her.*) Oh Catherine my light. My light.

   RUTH *and* MA *are frozen, witnessing* DOPHIE *as she stops and comes to listlessness.* RUTH *goes to her to gather her in.*

MA. Mammy?

RUTH. Dophie?

   There is no reply.

RUTH. It's Catherine, look. I'm here. Everything's all right. Look. Josephine?

   She doesn't look.

DOPHIE. I want to go home.

RUTH. So do I.

MA. Sure you are home Mammy. (*Indicating the signs.*) Look. (*To* RUTH.) So much for all my efforts.

RUTH. I wish it was as easy as a few signs. There's no map for this territory Mammy. Any of it.

MA (*taking* DOPHIE). I am doing my best Ruth. Best as I know how. She needs *peace*. (*To* RUTH.) Could you not have left her alone? The doctor says we're supposed to keep her orientated. Aware of what's going on around her.

RUTH. In that case maybe she's better off where she is then.

MA (*taking* DOPHIE's *hat off*). Time for another wee set, I think, ha? Rest first. Or maybe we'll go *out* to the hairdressers, eh, the two of us, a wee trip. Eh Mammy? (*To* RUTH.) And get rid of those suitcases, they're not helping.

RUTH. Trying to put me out as quick as you can again?

MA. Your decision Ruth. If it's what you want, I'm only trying to make things easier.

RUTH. This is *not* easy! Mammy *talk* to me! You've ignored me all day.

Nothing.

For God's sake Mammy the car is outside. Are you really going to let me just *go?*

Still nothing. RUTH *doesn't know what else to do. She lifts the suitcases.*

Ha! I used to wonder when I was away 'how do you take yourself out of the loop and still feel connected to something?' How was I so misguided?! I could go anywhere on the planet and *never* get myself extricated from this!

She heads for the door.

MA. Well at least you've banished any false notions of home that were holding you back before.

She sets DOPHIE *down at the table.* DOPHIE *sees her handbag sitting on top of it, lifts it down and arranges it on her lap. She sits up straight, smiling.*

DOPHIE. Are we going?

MA. Someone is.

DOPHIE. Oh good.

MA (*at* RUTH). With about as much notice for her departure as there was for her arrival.

RUTH. You're not exactly giving me much room to stay.

Beat.

Would you not like me to stay?

Beat.

If you let me go without resolving this Mammy, there's your future. (DOPHIE.)

Beat.

Can you not *try* and fix it?

MA. I wouldn't know where to begin. I'm not even sure what's broken anymore.

RUTH. Well if you don't know that. . . Look I've a month in Frankfurt. Give us both some cooling off time.

Beat.

You were afraid of me coming back weren't you? (*Pause.*) That's all right you know.

Beat.

MA. You'll be there on what would have been your wedding day then?

RUTH. I guess so. What a mess have I made.

MA. You had some help.

RUTH. Is that an apology?

Beat.

MA. Did you see your sister?

RUTH. I called into her at lunchtime to tell her I was going. I was informed she was 'out at a meeting'. Her coat was on the hat-stand. She never was any good at lying.

Beat.

I suppose there's not much point in trying to give her Catherine's money is there? (*Pause.*) Too little too late. Again.

MA. I should have thrown it into the grave with him. Buried it all right there.

DOPHIE. Bury me with it.

They both turn to look at her: she hasn't ruffled.

MA. I think she means funeral expenses.

RUTH. Something should be done with it. It should be exorcised.

MA. It'll sit in there and rot. (*The sideboard.*)

RUTH. But do we all have to rot with it?

Beat.

That same money bore down hard on both of us.

Beat.

We've that in common.

MA (*softening*). Maybe it's not too late with Matt?

RUTH. I'm calling him from Germany. Is it too late here?

Beat.

MA. No.

The car-horn blasts from outside. DOPHIE*'s hat is sitting on the table. She puts it on her head.*

RUTH. He can wait.

MA. He'll not wait forever Ruth.

The horn blasts again.

(*Afraid of melting.*) Please go. You know what I'm like about taxi fares.

Beat.

RUTH *goes to kiss* DOPHIE.

RUTH. I'll see you soon Nana. I promise.

DOPHIE *nods but keeps her eyes fixed forward, alert and excited.*

RUTH *stops at* MA *but neither can hug or speak.* RUTH *collects her bags.*

I'm off.

MA *nods.*

Exit RUTH.

MA *crumples in on herself. She goes and sits in the chair beside* DOPHIE, *still smiling and staring ahead, her hat on, her handbag neatly on her lap. Lights begin to fade. Car headlights cross.*

Beat.

DOPHIE. Are we nearly there yet?

Beat.

MA (*barely audible*). Nearly.

Curtain.

A Nick Hern Book

Midden first published in Great Britain in 2001
as an original paperback by Nick Hern Books Limited,
14 Larden Road, London W3 7ST

Midden © 2001 by Morna Regan

Morna Regan has asserted her right to be identified
as the author of this work

Typeset by Country Setting, Kingsdown, Kent CT14 8ES
Printed and bound in Great Britain by Biddles of Guildford

A CIP catalogue record for this book is available from
the British Library

ISBN 1 85459 656 X